D0887471

OSPREY AIRCRAFT OF THE ACES 119

F6F HELLCAT ACES
OF VF-9

SERIES EDITOR: TONY HOLMES

OSPREY AIRCRAFT OF THE ACES 119

F6F HELLCAT ACES OF VF-9

Edward M Young

OSPREY
PUBLISHING

Front Cover
Shortly after dawn on the morning of 17 February 1944, Task Force 58 sent off a fighter sweep over the Imperial Japanese Navy's bastion at Truk. That morning Lt(jg) Eugene Valencia was flying with his best friend Lt(jg) William Bonneau as part of Lt Charles Moutenot's division. As Valencia later recalled, 'our squadron was first over Truk, and it was a mighty exciting experience because we didn't know what to expect. The only maps we had were made from such high altitudes that they didn't show much. We didn't know the weapons nor the strength of the enemy at Truk as we had at Marcus Islands and Wake and Rabaul. But it didn't take long to find out. The Japs were surprised, but we soon had an "escort" of 80 Jap Zeros. They came at us from every angle. The confusion was terrific. The Japs threw up everything they had from fighters to seaplanes. We were shooting them down so fast the air was literally filled with parachutes. That, brother, was really something to see.'

A flight of Zero-sens jumped Moutenot's division, forcing the three pilots to take violent evasive action to escape. Valencia dove down to sea level, but found six to eight Zero-sens bracketing him. The Japanese fighters began making high-side runs on the Hellcat. On their third run, two Zero-sens pulled up ahead of Valencia, who quickly shot both of them down. Turning into the next attack, Valencia hit a third fighter in a head-on run and watched it crash into the sea. With 4.5 victories to his name prior to this engagement, Valencia 'made ace' with his three Zero-sen kills over Truk (*Cover artwork by Mark Postlethwaite*)

First published in Great Britain in 2014 by Osprey Publishing
PO Box 883, Oxford, OX1 9PL, UK
PO Box 3985, New York, NY 10185-3985, USA

E-mail: info@ospreypublishing.com

Osprey Publishing is part of the Osprey Group

© 2014 Osprey Publishing Limited

All rights reserved. Apart from any fair dealing for the purpose of private study, research, criticism or review, as permitted under the Copyright, Design and Patents Act 1988, no part of this publication may be reproduced, stored in a retrieval system, or transmitted in any form or by any means, electronic, electrical, chemical, mechanical, optical, photocopying, recording or otherwise without prior written permission. All enquiries should be addressed to the publisher.

A CIP catalogue record for this book is available from the British Library

ISBN: 978 1 78200 335 9
PDF e-book ISBN: 978 1 78200 336 6
ePub ISBN: 978 1 78200 337 3

Edited by Tony Holmes
Cover Artwork by Mark Postlethwaite
Aircraft Profiles by Jim Laurier
Index by Zoe Ross
Originated by PDQ Digital Media Solutions, UK
Printed in China through Asia Pacific Offset Limited

14 15 16 17 18   10 9 8 7 6 5 4 3 2 1

Osprey Publishing is supporting the Woodland Trust, the UK's leading woodland conservation charity, by funding the dedication of trees.

www.ospreypublishing.com

Acknowledgements
My sincere thanks to Lt Cdr Alison Shuler, US Navy, for her help in obtaining the war diaries of VF-9 and Carrier Air Group (CAG) Nine through the Freedom of Information Act. I would also like to thank the following individuals and their institutions for their help and support – the Naval Aviation History Office at the Naval History and Heritage Command in Washington, D.C.; Mr Hill Goodspeed and the volunteers at the National Naval Aviation Museum at Pensacola, Florida; Ms Holly Reed and her able staff at the Still Pictures Reference at the National Archives and Records Administration at Archives II, College Park, Maryland; Cdr Doug Siegfried of the Tailhook Association; and Mr John Little and Ms Katherine Williams at the Museum of Flight in Seattle, Washington. I would also like to express my thanks to my fellow Tuesday volunteers at the Museum of Flight, Ed Davies, Steve Ellis and Dennis Parks, for their support and encouragement.

CONTENTS

ORGANISATION, TRAINING AND FIRST COMBAT CRUISE

During World War 2 the US Navy developed a new means of projecting naval power that amounted to a revolution in naval warfare – the Fast Carrier Task Force. The carrier battles of 1942 between the Imperial Japanese Navy (IJN) and the US Navy proved that control of the sea required control of the air, and rendered the battleship and the battle line doctrine obsolete. Built up through American industrial power during 1942 and 1943, based on pre-war experiments and doctrine, but tried, tested and perfected in the early battles for the Gilbert Islands, attacks on Rabaul and the Marshall Islands, the Fast Carrier Task Force that emerged in early 1944 proved to be ideal for the Pacific War.

The multiple carrier task groups in the Fast Carrier Task Force, comprising three to four carriers in each task group, provided the US Navy with unprecedented power and mobility to range across the Pacific, penetrating the island barrier the Japanese had hoped to create, to strike at Japanese bastions and naval forces in the march across the Central Pacific. The deployment of the Fast Carrier Task Force during the final two years of the Pacific War represented a true paradigm shift, creating a new method of warfare.

The core elements of the Fast Carrier Task Force were the large *Essex*-class fleet carriers in the carrier task groups, supported by smaller *Independence*-class light carriers. The Fast Carrier Task Force's striking power came from the carrier air groups aboard the fleet carriers and the light carriers. Fortuitously for the US Navy, the design and construction of the *Essex*-class carriers coincided with the successful design and development of a new generation of carrier aircraft, namely the Grumman F6F Hellcat and TBF Avenger and the Curtiss SB2C Helldiver. With greater speed, range and armament than their predecessors, these three aeroplanes would progressively equip the carrier air groups on the fleet carriers, replacing the earlier Grumman F4F Wildcat, Douglas TBD Devastator and, after some time, Douglas SBD Dauntless.

But the construction of new fleet carriers, production of new aircraft and the development of new tactics and doctrine for carrier warfare took time. When the IJN launched its attack on Pearl Harbor on 7 December 1941, only five of the new *Essex*-class carriers were under construction, and two

'Murderer's Row' – five *Essex*-class carriers at Ulithi in early 1945. The *Essex*-class carriers formed the backbone of the Fast Carrier Task Force. During World War 2 VF-9 flew from USS *Essex* (CV-9), USS *Lexington* (CV-16) and USS *Yorktown* (CV-10) (*National Naval Aviation Museum*)

had had their keels laid down only a week before. The first production TBF Avenger would be delivered a month later, the first production model of the SB2C Helldiver would not arrive until June 1942 and the XF6F Hellcat would not make its first flight until that same month.

It was evident that the new carriers and the new generation of carrier aeroplanes to be flown from them would not arrive in quantity until later in 1943. In the interim, the US Navy faced the daunting task of recruiting and training the thousands of men that would be needed to man the ships and aircraft of its planned fleet. Entirely new carrier air groups had to be commissioned, organised, manned and trained for war, and then take their new aircraft and their new carriers off to do battle with the Japanese.

The first of the new, numbered carrier air groups to be formed was Carrier Air Group (CAG) Nine, commissioned on 1 March 1942 and assigned to the first of the new fleet carriers, USS *Essex* (CV-9). On its formation, CAG-9 consisted of four squadrons – Bombing Squadron Nine (VB-9), Scouting Squadron Nine (VS-9), Torpedo Squadron Nine (VT-9) and Fighting Squadron Nine (VF-9). Fighting Squadron Nine, like many of the US Navy's other World War 2 fighter squadrons, was a purely wartime creation, having had no pre-war antecedents. Most of the men who flew with the unit during the war, apart from the few most senior pilots, were new to Naval Aviation, having received their training as Naval Aviators in the months before or after the attack on Pearl Harbor. During the war these young men built an impressive record that saw VF-9 end the conflict as one of the US Navy's most successful fighter squadrons.

Apart from a brief first combat cruise flying F4F Wildcats in support of Operation *Torch* in November 1942, VF-9 achieved fame as a Hellcat squadron, flying the Grumman F6F during two combat cruises in the Pacific. The first US Navy unit to receive the F6F, VF-9 became the second-highest scoring Hellcat squadron of the war with 250.75 claims and produced the third-highest number of Hellcat aces – 20 of its pilots scored five or more victories while assigned to VF-9. Among the squadron's aces were

Lt(jg) Hamilton McWhorter, the first Hellcat ace, and Lt Eugene Valencia, who ended the war tied with Lt Cecil Harris as the second-highest scoring US Navy ace with 23 victories. During the Okinawa campaign in 1945, the division Valencia led became the US Navy's highest scoring division with a combined total of 42.5 victory claims. These victories were not without cost. In the course of VF-9's three combat cruises, the unit lost eight pilots killed in action and had a further six posted missing in action.

ORGANISATION AND TRAINING

Fighting Squadron Nine began life on 1 March 1942 as a small collection of pilots and aeroplanes, but fortunately with an experienced Naval Aviator in command. Lt Cdr John 'Jack' Raby, VF-9's first commander, was a Naval Academy graduate from the class of 1929 and an experienced Naval Aviator. He had spent three years as a fighter pilot with VF-3B embarked in USS *Langley* (CV-1), then completed two tours as an instructor at NAS Pensacola, Florida, before becoming Executive Officer of VF-8 aboard USS *Hornet* (CV-8). When Lt Cdr John Raby read out his orders as commander of VF-9, he had one lieutenant (junior grade) as his Executive Officer, six brand new ensigns, 162 enlisted men, five Brewster F2A-3 Buffalos and a single North American SNJ-3 trainer with which to commence the building of a future fighter squadron.

VF-9's first home was East Field at Naval Air Station (NAS) Norfolk, Virginia. Although the squadron had only five aircraft, training began immediately. It was not long before the squadron suffered its first fatality when Ens 'Artie' Buck went into a fatal spin at low altitude in one of the squadron's F2A-3s on 13 March 1942. Training and operational accidents would be a depressing but recurring event throughout the squadron's life.

Although intended to be equipped with the F4F Wildcat, the demands of the carrier fighter squadrons in the Pacific meant that newer units like VF-9 had to fly whatever they were given. It appears that for the first two months of its existence VF-9 rarely had more than six aeroplanes on strength, and for most of this period it had to rely on the F2A-3 – its Buffalos had previously served with VS-201 aboard the escort carrier USS *Long Island* (CVE-1). The first Wildcats, in the form of the earlier F4F-3 model, began to arrive in April 1942, but it was not until mid-May that the unit had more than a dozen aircraft assigned. Still, VF-9 was better off than its sister-squadrons in CAG-9, who for months had to make do with SNJ trainers or Vought OS2U-3 Kingfishers.

Newly minted ensigns, mostly fresh from Aircraft Carrier Training Groups, arrived steadily to build the squadron up to full strength. Ens Hamilton McWhorter, who joined VF-9 in late April 1942, was typical of the new pilots joining the squadron. McWhorter had learned to fly at university through the Civilian Pilot Training Program

Lt Cdr Jack Raby poses by one of VF-9's F4F-4 Wildcats on board USS *Ranger* (CV-4). He commanded VF-9 until his promotion to commander of CAG-9 in August 1943 (*80G-35053, Record Group 80, National Archives and Records Administration (NARA)*)

before joining the US Navy's V-5 Aviation Cadet Program in June 1941. Having completed his primary and basic flying training at NAS Pensacola, McWhorter was selected for fighters and went through a month's training on the F2A at NAS Opa-Locka near Miami, Florida, earning his wings and commission as an ensign on 9 February 1942.

McWhorter was then assigned to the Aircraft Carrier Training Group (ACTG) at NAS Norfolk, where he learned to fly the F4F Wildcat, did more training in air-to-air gunnery and practised carrier landings. He qualified as a carrier pilot by making eight landings on *Long Island*. McWhorter completed his ACTG training on 24 April 1942 and simply walked across the building the ACTG shared with VF-9 on East Field to join his new squadron, some ten months after enlisting in the US Navy.

Training was continuous and relentless, with pilots flying nearly every day, getting in three and sometimes more flights to practise formation flying, aerial gunnery and aerobatics. The training flights would often end with a tail chase, the flight leader putting the pilots through every manoeuvre he could think of. USAAF P-40s, flying out of nearby Langley Field, proved to be enthusiastic opponents in mock dogfights. Ferrying brand new F4F-4s out to the West Coast also proved a valuable and productive way for new ensigns to build up their flying hours, as did dawn-to-dusk anti-submarine patrols off the Virginia coast flown during June and July.

In late April Lt Hugh Winters, a Naval Academy graduate and experienced carrier flyer, as well as a future Hellcat ace and Carrier Air Group (CAG) commander, arrived to take over as Executive Officer, helping with the squadron's move to nearby NAS Oceana in early May. A month later the first F4F-4s arrived, gradually replacing the F4F-3s over the course of the summer. By early August VF-9 had 25 pilots and 20 Wildcats on hand.

After six months of hard training and waiting for *Essex* to be commissioned, the squadron's pilots were beginning to wonder when, and even if, they

One of VF-9's F4F-4 Wildcats lands aboard *Ranger* in the late summer of 1942. The squadron completed two short training cruises embarked in CV-4 prior to its participation in Operation *Torch* in November of that same year (*80G-20323, NARA*)

would finally get into the war. There had been a flurry of activity in late June when VF-9 had been alerted to move to NAS Quonset Point, Rhode Island, to transfer to the Royal Navy carrier HMS *Victorious* for transport to Malta, where the squadron would be land based to fight against the Luftwaffe, but this order was quickly cancelled. Another cause for excitement came in August when a small number of officers and enlisted men visited the Vought-Sikorsky plant at Stratford, Connecticut, to examine the new Vought F4U Corsair and receive instruction in its maintenance. The pilots were told that VF-9 would be the first US Navy squadron to convert to the Corsair once development testing had been completed.

Towards the end of the month the pilots received their first taste of real carrier operations when the squadron and 22 F4F Wildcats embarked in USS *Ranger* (CV-4) for a week's cruise to Quonset Point, conducting intensive flight operations along the way. A second ten-day cruise on *Ranger* followed in early September. Finally, at the end of the month, VF-9 was alerted to prepare to embark on *Ranger* for an extended period, destination unknown.

OPERATION *TORCH*

The US Navy's primary task in Operation *Torch* was to support the landing of American troops on the western coast of French Morocco, this force aiming to capture Casablanca and Port Lyautey. In September 1942 the US Navy organised Task Force (TF) 34 as part of the Western Naval Task Force, the vessels assigned to it transporting 35,000 troops and their supplies from the United States across the Atlantic to French Morocco.

Air support would be critical to the success of the invasion, as the Vichy air forces in the Casablanca region (comprising elements of the *Armée de l'Air* and the *Aéronavale*) could muster approximately 197 aircraft in defence of French Morocco. Amongst these machines were 46 Curtiss H-75A and 13 Dewoitine D.520 fighters in *Groupe de Chasse* (GC) I/5 and II/5 and 27 D.520s in *Flotille* 1F, as well as some 78 Loire et Olivier LeO 451, Douglas DB-7 and Martin M.167F medium bombers.

With the US Navy's surviving fleet carriers heavily committed to the conflict in the Pacific, *Ranger* was the only larger carrier available to TF 34. After an abbreviated shakedown period, four new *Sangamon*-class escort carriers were also assigned to the Task Force, three with their full complement of F4F Wildcats, SBD Dauntlesses and TBF Avengers and one to ferry 76 USAAF P-40s to North Africa, where they would be flown ashore to newly captured airfields. To increase the number of fighters available, *Ranger*'s carrier air group, CAG-4, left behind its torpedo-bomber squadron, VT-41, to make room for VF-9 with 27 F4F-4 Wildcats, giving the force a total of 103 fighters.

In an effort to maintain secrecy, the components of TF 34 left from different ports. On 2 October 1942, VF-9 and its 27 Wildcats joined VF-41 and VS-41 aboard *Ranger* in Norfolk, Virginia, and sailed for Bermuda, ostensibly for further training. Arriving at the island on 7 October, both fighter squadrons spent the next two weeks undertaking intensive training from *Ranger*'s flightdeck. Finally, on 25 October, CV-4 and the escort carriers set sail for French Morocco. *Ranger* and USS *Suwanee* (CVE-27) made up Task Group (TG) 34.2, covering the vital Center Attack Group, tasked with the capture of Casablanca.

To provide more flexibility in organising air strikes and combat air patrols (CAPs), the combined 54 Wildcats of VF-9 and VF-41 were divided into three 18-aeroplane squadrons, VF-9 and VF-41 each contributing nine fighters and pilots to form the third squadron, which the Naval Aviators dubbed 'VF-49'. Joining the main body of TF 34 in mid-Atlantic, *Ranger*'s fighter squadrons did no flying during the vessel's journey across the ocean, instead spending their time memorising maps of the invasion area and the location of all the French airfields. There was still a great deal of uncertainty about how the Vichy French would react to the American landings, the captain of *Ranger*, Capt C T Durgin, telling the pilots that they would know not long after taking off.

VF-9 went to war at 0615 hrs on 8 November 1942 when Lt Cdr John Raby led nine Wildcats aloft, quickly followed by nine more led by Lt Hugh Winters, to attack French airfields around Rabat at Rabat-Salé and Rabat-Ville. Shortly thereafter the SBDs of VS-41 and the 18 Wildcats of VF-41 took off for their targets, and then it was the turn of the 16 Wildcats of 'VF-49' under the command of Lt Mac Wordell, VF-41's executive officer and a future ace. Ens Marvin Franger, also a future ace, was flying as Raby's wingman on the mission that morning. At takeoff time, the pilots still did not know what reception they would receive. 'I got the takeoff signal and rolled down the deck into the black murk', Franger recalled, 'I finally got my 26 cranks in and my old wheels rolled up in my F4F. When I looked out over the horizon and I saw guns blazing, and I knew this was it, this was for keeps'.

Arriving over Rabat-Ville, Raby led his sections in repeated strafing runs across the airfield, destroying three H-75s. Nearby, Hugh Winters took one section down to strafe Rabat-Salé while the second section patrolled above. After making several runs across the airfield, and with no aerial opposition, Winters called down the five pilots in his second section, who added to the destruction. Winters reported that his sections had destroyed

Lt Cdr Jack Raby stands with the pilots of VF-9 on *Ranger*'s flightdeck just before Operation *Torch*. Ens Hamilton McWhorter is standing at far left (*80G-31315, NARA*)

four heavy bombers and ten medium bombers. In fact, the two sections had actually done even better, destroying nine LeO 451s from *Groupe de Reconnaissance* I/22 and 16 Potez 29s and four Farman 222 and 223 transports belonging to *Groupe de Transport* I/15.

Mac Wordell had led the combined VF-41/VF-9 formation on a patrol over the landings at Fedala. After cruising uneventfully overhead the landing beaches for 30 minutes, Wordell observed a French naval force of one light cruiser and

Pilots of VF-9 and VF-41 in their ready room await the order to man their aeroplanes in the early hours of 8 November 1942. The pilots dubbed their combined group 'VF-49'. Lt Jack Onstott of VF-9 stands in the centre of the back row wearing a tie, while Ens Hamilton McWhorter can be seen sitting in the back on the far right (*80G-30253, NARA*)

five destroyers heading out of Casablanca harbour. He led his sections down in a strafing attack in the face of heavy anti-aircraft fire. Lt Jack Onstott, leading two sections from VF-9, with Ens Hamilton McWhorter as his wingman, followed shortly after. Wordell's Wildcat was hit in the oil cooler, forcing him to break off the attack and head for the shore, where he made a successful crash landing. The other sections completed three more strafing runs, however, setting two of the destroyers on fire and forcing the French ships to reverse their course and return to Casablanca. In his memoir of his wartime service as a US Navy fighter pilot, Hamilton McWhorter recalled that on this, his first experience of combat, 'to say that I was frightened might not be entirely accurate, but the pucker factor was certainly up there'.

At 0945 hrs Lt Winters took off from *Ranger* with six other Wildcats to strafe the French airfield at Port Lyautey. Coming in on the airfield, the pilots saw seven D.520s being refuelled and re-armed, and in repeated strafing runs set all seven on fire. Flak claimed Ens Willie Wilhoite, who radioed 'They got me' just before his Wildcat hit the ground and exploded. Three other F4Fs were damaged during the attack and Lt Winters was slightly wounded. In the afternoon Lt Cdr Raby and Lt Winters led sections of Wildcats armed with two 100-lb bombs to patrol over the landing area. Raby and his three companions attacked four destroyers lying north of Casablanca harbour, each pilot strafing and dropping his bombs on one of the French ships, while Winters and his section bombed and strafed gun emplacements west of the city.

To the frustration of the VF-9 pilots, their compatriots in VF-41 monopolised the air combat on the first day of the invasion. Indeed, VF-9's only aerial action of the day was in all likelihood a tragedy, although this was unknown at the time. Following an urgent request for fighters to repel French air attacks, Lt Cdr Raby took off on his second mission of the morning with three other Wildcats to patrol the landing area up to Port Lyautey. Raby saw a twin-engined bomber flying off the coast that he identified as a LeO 451. Making a stern approach, Raby set the bomber's port engine on fire. Ens Marvin Franger followed Raby's attack, setting the bomber's starboard engine on fire and sending it crashing into the water. No French bombers were lost at that time in that area, however, and it appears that the aeroplane Raby and Franger shot down was an RAF Lockheed Hudson of No 223 Sqn flying out of Gibraltar.

VF-9's turn to engage the enemy in the air came the next day when, at 0730 hrs, Lt Cdr Raby took off with two sections of Wildcats on a CAP over the landing area at Fedala. With the ceiling down to 8000 ft, Raby saw a formation of French aircraft that he identified as 16 H-75s. This was a force from GC I/5 sent out to escort French bombers attacking the invasion force, the Vichy pilots aggressively engaging the F4Fs. Diving down in an overhead pass, Raby opened fire on the leader of the second section of eight H-75s, causing the French pilot to climb up into the clouds above. Following through the cloud, Raby came out to find another H-75 in front of him. Opening fire in a side approach, Raby's target exploded.

At the same time Ens Marvin Franger (again flying as Raby's wingman) made a head-on attack on another H-75, closing to point-blank range. 'He was coming directly toward the division', Franger remembered, 'so I headed directly towards him. We both made a head-on pass at each other, and he lost'. As the H-75 came in on him, Franger pushed the control column forward to get below the French fighter, pulling up and firing before his opponent could depress his guns. Future ace Ens Albert Martin also fired at this aeroplane, which burst into flames.

When several H-75s jumped on his tail, Lt Casey Childers, leading the second section, went into a tight spiral to throw them off. When he pulled out of his spin at 1000 ft Childers found an H-75 in front of him so he opened fire, sending it smoking down to crash below him. Future ace

An F4F-4 from VF-9 gets refuelled in between missions during Operation *Torch* (80G-30240, NARA)

Ens Lou Menard, who was Childers' wingman on this mission, had attacked a section of three H-75s to forestall their attack, setting one of the French fighters on fire and seeing it crash into the ground. Finally, another future ace, Lt(jg) Harold Vita, attacked an H-75 he saw coming out of a cloud, setting it on fire before it disappeared back into a cloud. Raby, Franger, Childers, Menard and Vita were all given credit for destroying one French fighter apiece, which was in fact the number of H-75s that GC I/5 lost in the encounter.

At noon Raby led 13 VF-9 Wildcats to attack the French airfield at Mèdouina, just east of Casablanca. Raby counted 15 fighters and five or six Douglas DB-7 bombers dispersed around the field and in front of hangars. He led his section down in a strafing pass, with Hugh Winters coming in with his section right after. With the aeroplanes widely dispersed, the VF-9 sections were forced to attack from several different directions. As he was making his fourth or fifth strafing run, Lt Edward Micka, leading the fourth section, pulled up over a DB-7 just as the French bomber, set on fire in a previous run, exploded. Micka's shattered Wildcat crashed into the ground, killing him instantly. The VF-9 fighters destroyed all the bombers and all but three of the fighters on the airfield.

Later that afternoon the squadron suffered its second loss of the day during a mission in support of the advance of American troops. Lt Cdr Raby was leading nine Wildcats on a patrol of the roads around Port Lyautey when they found a French convoy of trucks and tanks. He led his section down in a strafing attack, and on one of the passes Lt(jg) Stanton Amesbury was apparently shot down by anti-aircraft fire.

10 November proved to be the last day of real action for VF-9. During the morning the squadron flew three ground support missions in the area around Fedala, strafing columns of French trucks and other vehicles. At 1420 hrs Lt Cdr Raby took two sections to strafe French naval ships and anti-aircraft emplacements in Casablanca harbour in support of an attack by nine SBDs of VS-41 on the battleship *Jean Bart*. Raby led his section down from 14,000 ft to strafe *Jean Bart*, while the other section attacked the surrounding anti-aircraft guns, with the SBDs quickly following. The latter scored hits on the 35,000-ton battleship but failed to knock it out.

VF-9 had few opportunities for aerial combat during *Torch*. However, future ace Ens Louis Menard claimed a Hawk H-75A during a dogfight with French *Armée de l'Air* fighters on 9 November 1942 – the first of his nine victories with VF-9 and VBF-12 (*80G-31302, NARA*)

American troops inspect French Hawk H-75A fighters damaged in VF-9's strafing attack on Mèdouina airfield on 9 November 1942 (*Robert Lawson Collection, National Naval Aviation Museum*)

French ships under attack in Casablanca harbour on 10 November 1942. Lt Cdr Jack Raby led eight VF-9 Wildcats in a strafing attack just before the SBDs of VB-41 went in (*via the author*)

Later that afternoon Lt Winters led five Wildcats back to Casablanca harbour to strafe two French destroyers, with unknown results.

On 11 November VF-9 flew three uneventful CAPs. That morning the French forces around Casablanca had agreed to a ceasefire. With the end of hostilities, and with the risk of German submarine attack growing, *Ranger* was ordered to return to the USA, departing on 12 November. Stopping at Bermuda along the way, it reached Norfolk on 24 November 1942. VF-9 flew back to East Field, and the next day the men of the squadron went on five days' leave. Fighting Squadron Nine had successfully passed its first, albeit brief, combat test.

The pilots of VF-9 returned from leave on 1 December 1942 to learn of two significant changes to the squadron's composition and equipment. The carrier battles in the Pacific earlier in the year had demonstrated the vital need for the fleet carriers to have more fighters available for defence, as well as to provide escorts for the dive- and torpedo-bombers in the carrier air group. The US Navy duly authorised an increase in established strength for fighter squadrons from 27 aeroplanes to 36, and more pilots to man them. Over the next two months ten more Naval Aviators joined VF-9, among them experienced flyer Lt Herbert Houck and a younger pilot fresh from a brief stint as an instructor, Lt(jg) Eugene Valencia. Both men would play prominent roles in the squadron during its two combat cruises in the Pacific, achieving acedom along the way.

As well as welcoming new pilots, the personnel of VF-9 also learned that they would soon be replacing their Wildcats with a newer and more capable fighter – not the F4U Corsair as everyone had expected, but Grumman's new F6F Hellcat. Some of the men who had examined the Corsair at the Vought factory and learned of its capabilities were disappointed not to be trading in their F4Fs for the new Vought fighter, but the news that VF-9 would be the first US Navy squadron to acquire the Hellcat went some way to mollify them.

In mid-January 1943 Lt Cdr Raby and two other pilots travelled up to Grumman's Bethpage factory on Long Island to pick up some of the first Hellcats to come off the production line. The three new fighters arrived at NAS Oceana, Virginia, which had been home to VF-9 since early

December, on 16 January 1943 and were immediately put to use to check out every pilot in the squadron. In his memoir *The First Hellcat Ace*, Hamilton McWhorter recalled his introduction to the new F6F;

'My first flight in the Hellcat, on 23 January 1943, was an incredible experience. Being so much bigger than the Wildcat, it of course felt more substantial, more solid. The more powerful engine had a smoother purr to it as well. And everything was powered hydraulically. There was no more wrestling with the landing gear – cranking it up or down by hand and hoping not to bust a set of knuckles or break a wrist or crack a shin. When I "poured the coal" to the big new fighter I was amazed at how much power the engine produced. It seemed like the aeroplane just leaped off the ground – the takeoff roll was so short compared to the Wildcat's. And once airborne, the Hellcat seemed to want to climb and climb and climb. Best of all, it was a dream to fly – so stable and much easier to handle than the Wildcat. Landings were a snap as well. The landing gear struts were widely spaced, so there was little tendency to ground loop on landing. This was a *very* welcome change from the little Wildcat.'

Over the next several weeks pilots shuttled between Oceana and Bethpage to ferry newly made Hellcats back to their base. On one of these flights the squadron got a dramatic demonstration of the Hellcat's rugged construction. Flying a new F6F back to Oceana, Lt 'Casey' Childers had the engine quit while he was over the Pine Barrens in southern New Jersey. While his squadronmates watched from above, Childers took his Hellcat in for a crash landing, ploughing through the pine trees. When the aeroplane came to a stop, Childers got out and walked away unhurt.

By the end of February VF-9 had 21 Hellcats and only two Wildcats on strength. As more aeroplanes became available the pilots completed

Commissioned on 31 December 1942 as the first vessel in its class, *Essex* undertook its shakedown cruise with CAG-9 embarked during March 1943 after the Carrier Air Group's squadrons had completed their carrier qualifications on board (*Robert Lawson Collection, National Naval Aviation Museum*)

Lt Cdr Jack Raby's F6F-3 Hellcat on board CV-9. Raby made the first Hellcat landing on an *Essex*-class carrier on 17 February 1943. During VF-9's first and second combat cruises the CO was always assigned aeroplane No 1 (*80G-062934, NARA*)

VF-9 F6F-3 Hellcats practise carrier landings during the *Essex* shakedown cruise in March-April 1943. Returning to Norfolk from Trinidad, VF-9 lost Ens Charles Gerhardt when his F6F-3 went over the side of the ship and into the sea. The cockpit canopy slammed shut and Gerhardt could not get out (*80G-062938, NARA*)

all their required familiarisation training and began working on formation flying, aerial gunnery, combat tactics and field carrier landing practice. The pilots were pleased to find that the Hellcat was an excellent gun platform. Several found that their gunnery scores improved markedly over what they had achieved in the Wildcat. The real challenge was getting every pilot through carrier qualifications, but with its inherent stability the Hellcat proved to be exceptionally adept at landing on a carrier. Lt Cdr Raby made the first Hellcat carrier landing on the newly commissioned *Essex* on 17 February 1943. A little over three weeks later the rest of the squadron's pilots went out and completed their required eight carrier landings each without incident, becoming the first US Navy squadron to qualify in the Hellcat.

CAG-9 went aboard *Essex* in mid-March for the ship's shakedown cruise around Trinidad. As the squadron's Unit History described the initial weeks of the cruise, '95 per cent of the personnel aboard had never been to sea, and the initial air operations were fouled up considerably'. After two weeks of intensive air operations, 'chaos gradually gave way to order'. For part of the time CAG-9 went ashore to a British airfield on Trinidad and began training as a full group flying simulated air strikes. The shakedown cruise proved invaluable in building skills and coordination between the carrier and the CAG, and between the fighter, bomber and torpedo squadrons.

Returning to East Field on 9 April, the men of VF-9 made last-minute preparations prior to departing for their second combat cruise, destination unknown. The shakedown had uncovered some minor mechanical problems with the Hellcat, and these were hurriedly addressed while *Essex* itself underwent last-minute repairs. After a short leave, VF-9's 43 officers and 15 enlisted men and the squadron's 36 Hellcats moved to the dockside at Norfolk, where the F6F-3s were hoisted aboard *Essex*, joining the 36 SBD Dauntlesses of VB-9 and VB-19 (as VS-9 had been re-designated) and the 18 TBF Avengers of VT-9, all led by Cdr Charles Griffin. On 10 May 1943 *Essex* set sail. Once at sea Capt Donald B Duncan announced his ship's destination – Pearl Harbor and the Pacific.

SECOND COMBAT CRUISE

Essex arrived at Pearl Harbor on 31 May 1943, whereupon CAG-9 flew its aeroplanes to NAS Barbers Point. For the next two and a half months it maintained a programme of intensive training, flying from the naval air station and, during brief spells at sea aboard *Essex*, working on tactics and gunnery. During these weeks of training the squadron was introduced to the 'Thach Weave' – the defensive tactic Lt Cdr John Thach had developed to counter the Japanese A6M Zero-sen's superior manoeuvrability. The pilots practised the manoeuvre in two-aeroplane sections and in four-aeroplane divisions until it became second nature.

Several command changes took place while the squadron was undergoing training. In mid-July, now-Lt Cdr Hugh Winters returned to the USA to take command of VF-19, a new Hellcat squadron. Recently promoted Lt Cdr Herbert Houck, who, two weeks earlier, had survived a mid-air collision, replaced Winters as Executive Officer. On 13 August, shortly before VF-9 left Pearl Harbor for its first combat, Cdr Griffin was promoted to become Air Officer on *Essex* and Lt Cdr John Raby moved up to become CAG Commander. Lt Cdr Philip Torrey, an Academy graduate and commander of VF-22 on board USS *Independence* (CVL-22), was transferred in to take command of VF-9.

While *Essex* and CAG-9 continued training, more new carriers arrived at Pearl Harbor to rebuild the US Navy's Pacific Fleet. During July USS *Yorktown* (CV-10), USS *Lexington* (CV-16) and three of the new

The pilots of VF-9 at NAS Barbers Point, Hawaii, in June 1943. Future VF-9 aces Lt(jg)s Marvin Franger, William Bonneau, Eugene Valencia and Hamilton McWhorter are stood in the middle row, second, sixth, seventh and ninth from the left (*via the author*)

Hellcats believed to be from VF-9 on *Essex* test their guns prior to the first strike on Marcus Island. The F6Fs carried large national insignia with a red surround on the sides of the fuselage (*80GK-678, NARA*)

light carriers, *Independence*, USS *Princeton* (CVL-23) and USS *Belleau Wood* (CVL-24) reached Hawaii, creating a potent weapon for the newly created Central Pacific Force, as the Fifth Fleet was then called. But it was a new and untried weapon. None of the *Essex*-class fleet carriers or the *Independence*-class light carriers had been in combat. There were many issues to be resolved around carrier doctrine relating to the most effective carrier formation, and whether carriers should operate singly, as pre-war carrier doctrine dictated, or in multi-carrier groups.

When supporting amphibious operations, a debate raged over whether the carriers should be tied to the landing areas to provide close air support, or be freed to use their striking power against other Japanese bases. There were questions on how well the new carrier air groups would perform with their new aircraft, and especially how well the Hellcat would fare against the vaunted Japanese Zero-sen.

By the summer of 1943 there was at least an agreement on the general strategy to be pursued against Japan. After much debate between the US Army and the US Navy, the American Joint Chiefs of Staff had agreed on a two-pronged advance across the Pacific. In the Southwest Pacific Gen Douglas MacArthur and Adm William Halsey would push the Japanese out of the Solomons, the Bismarck Islands and New Guinea, before pressing on to the Philippines. In the Central Pacific, Adm Chester Nimitz would command an advance west along the island chains, capturing the Gilbert Islands, the Marshall Islands, the Carolines and the Marianas. The ultimate goal of both drives was to establish American forces in the Philippines, Formosa or along the China coast in order to cut Japan off from its sources of raw materials in Southeast Asia.

But with the landings on the Gilbert Islands scheduled for November 1943, the first order of business was to break in the new carriers and their air groups. Adm Nimitz decided to use several of his newly arrived carriers in a series of hit-and-run strikes on some of the nearer Japanese island bases to give his sailors and airmen, and their commanders, valuable experience.

The first target was Marcus Island, 1568 miles northwest of Midway Island and only 1100 miles from Japan. Marcus had a small garrison and an airfield for Japanese patrol aeroplanes. *Essex* joined *Yorktown* and *Independence* as part of TF 15 under the command of Rear Adm Charles Pownall for the raid. The plan was to make a quick strike on the island and then withdraw back to Pearl Harbor. On the way, the carriers tried out a new multi-carrier cruising formation, with all three vessels in the centre of the formation surrounded by their battleship, cruiser and destroyer escorts to provide anti-aircraft protection.

Coming in from the north, TF 15 launched its aeroplanes on the morning of 31 August 1943. VF-9 flew four missions that day, escorting the dive- and torpedo-bombers of VB-9 and VT-9 to bomb the airfield and installations on the island. Lt Cdr Torrey led off the first mission at 0530 hrs, taking four divisions as escort for the SBDs. Torrey went in first with two divisions in a long strafing run across the island, shooting at anti-aircraft flashes. After the SBDs had completed their bombing runs, the second two divisions went down to strafe. Lt Cdr Houck led two divisions on the second mission, escorting the TBFs of VT-9. With no air opposition Houck took his Hellcats down to strafe gun emplacements, hangars and other airfield installations.

A photograph from the same series as the shot on page 19 showing a Hellcat being re-loaded during the test firing (*National Archives via the Tailhook Association*)

Torrey took the third mission later in the morning, and Houck the last, launching at 1235 hrs. Repeated strafing runs by VF-9, *Yorktown*'s VF-5 and VF-22 from *Independence* (both units were also equipped with F6F-3s) left large fires burning among the airfield installations. Around a dozen aeroplanes were left on fire, including seven to eight twin-engined bombers. The raid was judged a success, having been a worthwhile test of the carriers and their air groups.

Returning to Pearl Harbor after the Marcus Island raid, VF-9 spent a month devoted to more training. In the interim, TF 15 with *Lexington* and the light carriers *Princeton* and *Belleau Wood* went out to attack Tarawa, in the Gilbert Islands chain, in another hit-and-run training strike. In consultation with his staff, Adm Nimitz then planned a third practice mission – a two-day strike against Wake Island. This would involve six carriers, which was the largest American carrier formation assembled to date. Designated TF 14 under Rear Adm Alfred Montgomery, *Essex*, *Yorktown*, *Independence* and *Belleau Wood* formed one carrier group, with *Lexington* and the newly arrived USS *Cowpens* (CVL-25) forming the second. On 29 September 1943 VF-9 left Pearl Harbor on board *Essex* as part of TG 14.5, heading for Wake Island.

Marcus Island comes under attack by carrier-based aircraft from TF 15 on 31 August 1943 (*80G-474376, NARA*)

As the Japanese base closest to Pearl Harbor, Wake Island had been provided with a stronger defence than Marcus Island. Earlier in the year the IJN had moved the 252nd Kokutai (air group) to the Marshall Islands with its Zero-sen fighters. Headquartered on the island of Roi, in the Marshalls, the 252nd Ku had sent two buntai (sections) to Wake to protect the island from air attack,

A photograph taken shortly after the attack on Wake Island on 5 October 1943. VF-9 had its first encounter with the much-vaunted Japanese Zero-sen overhead Wake Island during this operation, claiming four shot down (*80G-85198, NARA*)

principally from USAAF B-24 bombers. On the morning of 5 October 1943 (the date set for the first American carrier strike) the 252nd Ku had around 26 Zero-sens available. Rear Adm Montgomery's plan was to close to around 90 miles from Wake and launch his first air strikes just before dawn so as to arrive over the island as the sun rose for maximum surprise.

VF-9's mission on the morning of 5 October was to escort CAG-9's dive- and torpedo-bombers and defend them against air attack, and to strafe enemy installations on the island. Lt Cdr Torrey took three divisions on the first mission, with future ace Lt(jg) Mayo 'Mike' Hadden leading the second division and Lt Casey Childers the third. The divisions took off at 0445 hrs in the pre-dawn darkness. With so many other carrier aircraft milling around before heading out to the same target, making the rendezvous with the VB and VT aircraft was practically impossible, so the three divisions proceeded separately toward the island at an altitude of 500 ft. Around 15 to 20 miles from Wake the Hellcats climbed to 7000 ft, where they joined up with their charges.

Flying in Hadden's division, Lt(jg) Hamilton McWhorter looked down to see a 'Zeke' (the Allied codename for the Zero-sen) flying below the bomber formation in the opposite direction. Fearing that the 'Zeke' pilot would pull up in an Immelmann turn to come in behind the bombers, McWhorter performed a right-hand turn to dive down on the enemy fighter. When part way through his turn he was astonished to see the 'Zeke' coming at him, guns firing, at his same altitude – this was McWhorter's first experience of the A6M's exceptional manoeuvrability. Knowing that the Hellcat could easily out-dive a 'Zeke', McWhorter did a 'split-S' at full throttle to escape. Sobered by his experience, McWhorter climbed back up to rejoin his division.

When the VF-9 divisions finally arrived over Wake, the islands were still in darkness. Torrey's and Childers' divisions went down separately to strafe the airfield, firing at buildings and aircraft revetments they could just make out in the early dawn light. Pulling up after their strafing runs, they ran into around a dozen Zero-sens flying above them. Alerted to the incoming raid, the 252nd Ku had put up 26 Zero-sens to intercept the 100 American carrier aircraft attacking the island. The VF-9 pilots reported that the IJN pilots attacking them were aggressive and used their superior altitude to their advantage.

Flying above the island, and temporarily separated from his division, Lt Cdr Torrey saw a 'Zeke' above and to the left of him, diving in to attack. Torrey turned into the attack and fired a long burst at the fighter, which went into a spin. Another VF-9 pilot saw a Zero-sen dive into the sea shortly thereafter, and Torrey was later given credit for one 'Zeke' destroyed. Still on his own, Torrey had two more 'Zekes' latch onto his tail. They kept up their attacks for several more minutes, forcing Torrey to take evasive action and use nearby clouds as cover to escape.

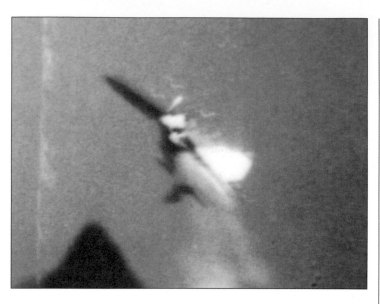

A Zero-sen goes down over Wake under the guns of Lt G C Bullard of VF-6 (this unit fought alongside VF-9 over Wake on 5 October 1943). The Hellcat's superior performance came as a nasty shock to the IJN's fighter pilots (*80G-85200, NARA*)

Meanwhile, Lt(jg) Mike Hadden and his division had been circling above Wake at around 23,000 ft, acting as high cover and waiting for dawn so they could identify their targets while keeping an eye out for enemy fighters. Seeing two 'Zekes' coming in to attack a formation of Hellcats below them, Hadden and his wingman, Lt(jg) Jack Kitchen, went after the fighters, only to have two more 'Zekes' come down to bounce them. Fortunately, the 'Zekes' misjudged their approach and missed Hadden and Kitchen. As Hadden recalled years later;

'We started turning toward them and they started turning toward us. All of sudden that circle kept getting larger and larger, so I thought, "Oh boy, I got him, I got him now!" I was way out of range, however – so far out of range that I was shooting with what I thought was the proper lead on the lead aircraft, but the second aeroplane blew up!'

The lead 'Zeke' pulled up and disappeared, while the second machine went down smoking, out of control, and exploded when it hit the sea. Hadden later received credit for the victory – his first. While watching his victim crash, Hadden's lead 'Zeke' came around to attack him. 'We were kind of excited', Hadden subsequently recalled. 'I made a big orbit watching this guy go down. I had just completed a 360 when all hell broke loose. That first Zero was sitting right on my tail. I could hear the 7.7 mm rounds rattling on the back of the armour plate like popcorn, and there were holes all of a sudden appearing in the aeroplane. This guy had me bore-sighted'. The 'Zeke' was outturning Hadden and closing in fast to get in a solid burst of fire. In an instant five 20 mm cannon shells slammed into the Hellcat and 7.7 mm machine gun fire riddled the fighter. The cannon shells hit Hadden's port and starboard wings, damaged his right elevator and stabiliser, knocked ten inches off the top of his rudder and entered the front of the aeroplane ahead of the cockpit, shattering the oil tank. Fragments from one of the shells wounded Hadden in the leg.

Desperate to escape, the Hellcat pilot remembered someone saying that if you started a turn with a 'Zeke', and if you could get it committed, you could reverse the turn and the 'Zeke', which had a poorer roll rate at higher speeds, would not be able to follow. Hadden went into a turn, and when the 'Zeke' started to follow, he whipped around in the opposite direction. He and Kitchen, who remarkably had stayed with him, escaped with a high-speed dive and returned to *Essex*. Because of the damage to his Hellcat, Hadden circled above the carrier until the rest of the aeroplanes had recovered. He came in and landed with no flaps and no hydraulics, but caught a wire. The maintenance crew found that Hadden had only a gallon and a half of oil left in the tank.

As he flew over Wake, Hamilton McWhorter repeatedly resorted to steep diving turns to escape his attackers. After his initial encounter with the 'Zeke' en route to the target, a second enemy fighter attacked McWhorter from above, forcing him to dive away. Seeing another 'Zeke' above him after he recovered from his dive, McWhorter pulled up to attack, only to have the 'Zeke' turn inside him and almost get onto his tail before he could dive away. Twenty minutes later, while patrolling above the island with another Hellcat from VF-9, McWhorter and his wingman were attacked from above by yet another 'Zeke', forcing them into another fast dive. Pulling out at 4000 ft, McWhorter saw a 'Zeke' directly ahead of him. He made a high stern attack, setting the fighter on fire and sending it down to explode when it hit the sea for his first victory. Shortly thereafter McWhorter fired a solid burst at another A6M that immediately ducked into a cloud – he received credit for a 'Zeke' probably destroyed.

VF-9 carried out three flights to Wake that day, but its pilots failed to encounter any more Japanese fighters. The divisions satisfied themselves instead with strafing runs on installations and anti-aircraft positions across the islands, making a series of high-speed passes. They were opposed by small-calibre anti-aircraft and machine gun fire, which holed several aeroplanes.

Lt(jg) Mayo 'Mike' Hadden, who had a narrow escape over Wake when a 'Zeke' jumped him. Hadden achieved all eight of his victories flying with VF-9. Remaining in the US Navy after the war, he later commanded USS *Hornet* (CV-12) and retired as a rear admiral (*via the author*)

An F6F-3 from VF-9 showing the squadron insignia and one victory marking beneath the cockpit. During its second combat cruise VF-9 appears to have had a practice of putting victory markings on Hellcats that were used to down enemy aircraft (*80G-217624, NARA*)

The carriers went back to Wake the next day to attack through rain squalls and heavier cloud cover. As Lt(jg) Eugene Valencia was making a strafing run, a 'Zeke' unaccountably dove directly ahead of him and through his stream of fire. Valencia received credit for a 'Zeke' damaged in his first aerial encounter. The poorer weather apparently caused the loss of Lt(jg) R M McGann, who was flying with Lt(jg) Marvin Franger as escort to a TBF. Entering a storm cloud, Franger succumbed to vertigo and nearly crashed into the sea. McGann did not return from the mission, having probably crashed due to the same cause.

Yorktown's VF-5 took top honours for the Wake strike, claiming 16 'Zekes' shot down – other fighter squadrons, including VF-9, claimed a further 15 destroyed. The aerial combats over Wake gave proof of the Hellcat's superiority over the Zero-sen. VF-9's first encounter with the 'Zeke' was a success, with claims for four shot down, one probable and one damaged without loss, although Mayo Hadden's Hellcat had been extensively damaged.

This experience taught the VF-9 pilots some key lessons as follows. Firstly, the 'Zeke' was more manoeuvrable than the Hellcat and could easily turn inside an F6F. Secondly, steep high-speed diving turns, especially to the right, were an effective evasive manoeuvre as the 'Zeke' could not match the Hellcat's speed or control in a dive. Thirdly, the Hellcat's armament was far more effective than the 'Zeke's'. Fourthly, the Hellcat had far better protection in its armour and rugged construction. Mayo Hadden's fighter had taken heavy punishment, yet it brought him back to the carrier, while the 'Zekes' encountered repeatedly exploded under fire from their opponents.

The aerial battle over Wake on 5 October proved to be a disaster for the 252nd Ku. The air group lost 16 Zero-sen fighters in combat against the Hellcats, and had a further three pilots return to base wounded, while claiming 14 American aircraft shot down. The loss of WO Toshiyuki Sueda, a China veteran and one of the most experienced Zero-sen pilots in the air group, was a blow to morale, as was the realisation that the new Hellcat fighter clearly out-performed the Zero-sen.

RABAUL

Essex returned to Pearl Harbor after the Wake strike and VF-9 took up residence again at Barbers Point, but only briefly. The Central Pacific Force was preparing for Operation *Galvanic*, the invasion of Tarawa, scheduled for 20 November 1943. As TF 50, the five fleet carriers and four light carriers available to Rear Adm Pownall were organised into three task groups (task groups were subordinate to task forces). *Essex* would be part of TG 50.3 with *Independence* and the new USS *Bunker Hill* (CV-17).

Within ten days of returning to Pearl Harbor VF-9 embarked in *Essex* and set sail for the South Pacific, and specifically the island of Espiritu Santo, with a new CAG CO. At a high-spirited CAG-9 party to celebrate the success of the Wake strike a few days after *Essex's* return, Cdr John Raby had broken his leg. VT-9's CO, Lt Cdr Paul Emrick, was duly made acting CAG Commander. One of the reasons for heading for Espiritu Santo was to rehearse the impending invasion of Tarawa, but upon its arrival on 5 November, CAG-9 learned that the invasion rehearsal had been cancelled. Instead, TG 50.3 had been re-assigned to Adm Halsey for strikes on the Japanese base at Rabaul, in New Guinea.

During 1943 Allied forces had steadily moved up the Solomon Islands chain, with the ultimate objective of destroying the Japanese air and naval stronghold at Rabaul, on New Britain, and thus break the enemy's hold on the Bismarck Archipeligo off the northeastern coast of New Guinea. In the early autumn the Joint Chiefs of Staff approved Adm Halsey's plan to establish airfields on the island of Bougainville that would bring Rabaul in range of Allied fighters and medium bombers. Halsey's planning staff decided to capture an isolated section of the west coast of Bougainville at Cape Torokina, in Empress Augusta Bay, and scheduled the invasion for 1 November 1943. In the weeks leading up to D-Day Gen George Kenny's Fifth Air Force launched a series of heavy raids on Rabaul, attacking Japanese airfields and shipping.

The US Navy's growing strength in the Central Pacific and Allied progress up the Solomons presented Japan's Imperial Headquarters with a dilemma. How and where to defend against the next Allied attack? In late September Imperial Headquarters issued its 'New Operational Policy', which basically called for a determined defence of all Japanese positions so as to gain time to rebuild before taking the offensive in 1944. Holding Rabaul was vital to this defensive policy. The IJN still hoped to engage the US Pacific Fleet in a decisive battle, and had moved the Combined Fleet out of its anchorage at Truk following the raid on Wake Island in the hope of engaging TF 14 in battle. However, when no invasion of Wake followed the 5 October attack, the Combined Fleet returned to Truk.

Instead, Adm Mineichi Koga, Commander in Chief of the Combined Fleet, decided to strip his carrier fleet of its entire air strength so as to reinforce the 11th Koku Kantai (11th Air Fleet) on Rabaul. At the end of October the air groups of the 1st Koku Sentai (1st Air Flotilla) – 82 A6M Type 0 fighters ('Zekes'), 45 D3A Type 99 carrier dive-bombers ('Vals'), 40 B5N Type 97 carrier torpedo-bombers ('Kates') and six D4Y Type 2 carrier reconnaissance aeroplanes ('Judys') – from the carriers *Zuikaku*, *Shokaku* and the *Zuiho* moved to Rabaul to join approximately 200 IJN aircraft stationed there. The 1st Koku Sentai arrived in Rabaul on 1 November 1943 – the day American forces invaded Bougainville.

When the Combined Fleet learned of the landings, Adm Koga sent a force of heavy and light cruisers and destroyers to attack the ships of Halsey's invasion force. On 5 November the small carrier force of USS *Saratoga* (CV-3) and *Princeton*, attacked Rabaul, severely damaging several cruisers and sending them back to Truk. Halsey had previously asked Adm Nimitz for carrier reinforcements in order to launch even heavier attacks against Rabaul so as to knock the base out once and for all. Nimitz complied, sending Task Group 50.3 to Halsey.

Essex anchored in Pallikulo Bay, off Espiritu Santo, on 5 November. Three days later Task Group 50.3 sailed for the attack on Rabaul. The plan was to have land-based air forces attack Rabaol on 9 and 10 November to weaken enemy air strength before the carriers launched their attacks on 11 November. *Saratoga* and *Princeton* (as TF 38) were scheduled to strike Rabaul from the north at 0800 hrs, taking off from a position northwest of Bougainville, while Task Group 50.3 was due to come in at 0930 hrs from the south, launching from a position to the southwest of the island. Land-based US Navy fighter squadrons (VF-17 with F4U Corsairs and VF-33 with F6F Hellcats) would provide a CAP over the carriers.

As often happened, the sequence of events did not go quite as planned. The preliminary strikes did not come off due to poor weather, so the carrier strikes faced the full force of the Japanese aircraft at Rabaul, but fortuitously the strike force from TF 38 was an hour late and the strike force from TG 50.3 30 minutes early, so the formations effectively attacked the target simultaneously.

All three of TG 50.3's Carrier Air Groups began launching at 0645 hrs when the force was 226 miles from Rabaul. CAG-9 sent out 28 SBDs from VB-9 and 18 TBFs from VT-9, with 29 F6Fs from VF-9 as

Japanese shipping in the harbour at Rabaul comes under attack during the 11 November 1943 raid (*80G-204661, NARA*)

escort. Lt Cdr Torrey led 12 of the fighters as escort to the SBDs, with Lt Casey Childers and Lt Mayo Hadden leading the other two divisions. Lt Cdr Houck took 13 Hellcats as escort to the TBFs, with Lts Charles Moutenot and Jack Kitchen as his division leaders. The remaining four Hellcat pilots provided a close escort for the CAG Commander's TBF, which would photograph the results of the strike.

Some 40 miles out from Rabaul, with the fighter escort weaving above the bombers, the TG 50.3 formation picked up an escort of eight to ten enemy fighters, who followed the carrier aeroplanes into the target area. Heading west along St George's Channel between New Ireland and New Britain, the formation ran into a rain squall, but came out into the clear again as they approached Blanche Bay – the body of water that led to Simpson Harbour, the main anchorage at Rabaul. The pilots could see Japanese shipping in the harbour, and more ships heading out in an attempt to reach the cover of rain squalls to the east. Over the radio they could hear aircraft from *Saratoga* and *Princeton* going in to attack. Lt Cdr Paul Emrick, acting commander of CAG-9, ordered one-third of the force to attack ships in Simpson Harbour, while the remaining two-thirds went for the ships trying to escape the attack. There to meet them were 35 'Zekes' from the 1st Koku Sentai, 24 from the 204th Kokutai and 19 from the 201st Kokutai.

Employing standard escort tactics, Torrey had his three divisions circle the dive-bombers as they began their attacks from 13,000 ft down on the Japanese ships below. When the last SBD entered its dive, Torrey led his division down, with Childers and Hadden following with their fighters, to prevent the numerous 'Zekes' flying above the formation from going after the SBDs. As the dive-bombers pulled out of their dives and retired at low level, the Hellcats joined up with the SBD formations and began scissoring over the bombers. The 'Zekes' had tailed the Dauntlesses and Hellcats down, and as they recovered from their dives the Japanese fighters came in to make stern attacks. The attacks persisted until the CAG-9 aeroplanes were well out to sea and away from Rabaul.

In the running fight that followed, VF-9 pilots claimed 14 'Zekes' shot down while protecting the bombers, for the loss of one pilot. The attacks were so numerous that the Naval Aviators could often do no more than drive off an attacking A6M and then quickly return to escorting the SBDs and TBFs on their withdrawal. Several pilots found that by using their combat flaps they could manoeuvre with a 'Zeke' for a short period, gaining on it in steep climbs at low altitude. And as the pilots had discovered so spectacularly over Wake, the six 0.50-cal machine guns fitted in the Hellcat's wings proved devastating against the lightly armoured 'Zekes'.

Lt Cdr Torrey and his wingman turned into one attack, and in a high-side run the former hit a 'Zeke' in its vulnerable wing fuel tanks. The fighter burst into flames and crashed into the water. A few minutes later Torrey's wingman shot a 'Zeke' off his leader's tail with a solid burst into the engine and wing roots, the 'Zeke' diving away in flames. In fending off other attacks, Torrey claimed another 'Zeke' as a probable.

Future ace Lt Armistead 'Chick' Smith knocked down two 'Zekes' with head-on attacks for his first kills. Going after several enemy fighters as they made runs on the SBDs, Smith targeted one 'Zeke' as is closed on the dive-bombers, setting it on fire and sending it down into the sea. Turning into another attacking 'Zeke', Smith got a good burst into its fuselage as the pilot pulled up and over him. Although no flames or explosions were apparent, this 'Zeke' was seen to crash into the sea too.

Recovering from his dive and heading for the rendezvous point, Lt Casey Childers looked back behind him to check on his wingman, Ens Robert Kaap, only to see Kaap's Hellcat on fire. A 'Zeke' had latched onto its tail and hit the Hellcat hard with 20 mm cannon fire. Kaap successfully ditched, but in the midst of the aerial battle all around no one could circle him and was posted missing in action.

As Lt Hadden's division pushed over to cover the dive-bombers in their attack runs, it went through a heavy rain squall and became separated from the SBDs. Lt(jg) Hamilton McWhorter and his wingman, Lt(jg) William Gehoe, also became separated from Hadden in the clouds. Coming out in the clear, McWhorter saw a line of Japanese warships ahead of him and immediately started in on a strafing run against a *Mogami*-class heavy cruiser. Climbing up and heading to the rendezvous point after surviving his attack, McWhorter noticed an aerial battle going on over a Japanese airfield south of the harbour, with 'Zekes' and Hellcats in fierce combat. Although he was on his own and without a wingman McWhorter headed for the fight.

During the morning strike on Rabaul on 11 November 1943, Lt(jg) Hamilton McWhorter and his wingman, Lt(jg) William Gehoe, claimed four 'Zekes' between them. McWhorter would get his fifth kill eight days later to become the first Hellcat ace (*via the author*)

Seeing a 'Zeke' on the tail of a Hellcat, he came in from the starboard quarter and set the fighter on fire. Closing in on another 'Zeke' ahead of him, McWhorter was startled to hear bullets hitting his Hellcat. As he later wrote, 'the noise was as if I had been standing inside a tin shed and someone had thrown a handful of rocks against the outside of it. It stung my ears, and I could feel the aeroplane vibrate as machine gun bullets slammed into it'. McWhorter had made the mistake of concentrating on his next target instead of keeping a lookout. He turned to see two 'Zekes' coming in on his tail, guns firing. He quickly pulled his Hellcat into a hard diving turn to escape. As he dove away, he caught sight of another 'Zeke' ahead of him. Seeing the Hellcat approach, the Japanese pilot pulled up in a steep climb, but McWhorter followed and was actually out-climbing the 'Zeke' when he opened fire with a 90-degree deflection shot, hitting the fighter, which immediately burst into flames.

Meanwhile, Lt(jg) William Gehoe, McWhorter's wingman, had accounted for two 'Zekes' on his own, one in a beam attack and one in a head-on run.

Lt Cdr Houck led his divisions down to escort the VT-9 Avengers in their attacks on the Japanese ships. They targeted an IJN cruiser, firing on the ship as the TBFs made their torpedo runs and then escorting the Avengers out of the harbour. As the formation raced out of Simpson Harbour following the attack, six or seven 'Zekes' jumped the aircraft from above. Lt(jg) Louis Menard turned into the attack, climbing up and opening fire on one of the 'Zekes'. The fighter he had targeted turned to the right, but Menard turned with him and continued firing as he came in on the 'Zeke' from astern, setting the Japanese fighter on fire and watching it crash into the sea.

Flying as the second section in Lt Moutenot's division, future aces Lt(jg)s Bill Bonneau and Eugene Valencia also became separated from the rest of their division when they went through a rain squall. Coming out, they saw a Japanese cruiser and a destroyer manoeuvring to escape the torpedo attacks. They duly made three strafing runs on these ships before breaking off their attacks when they saw some TBFs from *Bunker Hill* on their way out of the harbour. Quickly joining up with the Avengers, Bonneau and Valencia were soon called on to protect the TBFs from a pair of 'Zekes' that approached the torpedo-bombers from the right. The leading 'Zeke' turned to the left upon spotting the two Hellcats that were heading for them, but Bonneau managed to get onto the fighter's tail and continued firing until the A6M crashed into the sea.

Valencia, meanwhile, had seen the second 'Zeke' making another run on the TBFs and he went after it. The 'Zeke' pilot spotted the approaching Hellcat and started to climb away, but Valencia had no difficulty following the fighter in the climb. Getting off a long burst as he chased after the 'Zeke', Valencia saw the A6M's port wing burst into flame. He closed on the Japanese fighter, still firing, and the 'Zeke' exploded.

These were Bonneau's and Valencia's first aerial victories of the war, but not their only victories of the day.

Returning to *Essex*, the aeroplanes of CAG-9 were refuelled and re-armed in preparation for a second strike on Rabaul. The Carrier Air Group began taking off again at 1328 hrs, 16 TBFs from VT-9 departing first, followed by 31 Hellcats of VF-9. At this point in the launch evolution a Japanese air attack interrupted proceedings.

During the morning attack the Japanese command on Rabaul had recognised immediately that the American dive- and torpedo-bombers could only have come from aircraft carriers, and so prepared a counter-attack against the task force. The 1st Koku Sentai sortied 27 'Val' dive-bombers and 14 'Kate' torpedo-bombers, with an escort of 33 Zero-sen fighters the formation was possibly accompanied by several 'Judy' carrier reconnaissance aircraft too. Indeed, several Hellcat pilots subsequently submitted claims for 'Tony' fighters, which may have been an error in aircraft recognition for the Kawasaki Ki-61 Type 3 Hien was inline-engined like the D4Y1. An additional 32 Zero-sens from the 253rd Kokutai were also dispatched as escorts, but they failed to find the target and returned to Rabaul.

The Japanese attack came in four waves, the first at 1356 hrs from an estimated 32 'Vals' against all three of TG 50.3's carriers. Two minutes

Essex comes under attack from Japanese dive-bombers off Rabaul on 11 November 1943 (*Record Group 38, Box 345, Carrier Air Group Nine, NARA*)

later a second wave of nine 'Vals' went after *Bunker Hill*. Then at 1403 hrs the first group of 'Kates' came in, apparently with several Mitsubishi G4M Type 1 attack bombers (codenamed 'Betty'), quickly followed by another 'Kate' formation. The 'Vals' completed their attacks before the defending fighters could reach them, but fortunately without damaging any of the carriers. The Hellcats intercepted the 'Kates' beyond the TG 50.3's destroyer screen, however, and disrupting their attack.

As soon as *Essex* was targeted by the 'Vals' the launch stopped. The torpedo-bombers, already airborne, were ordered to circle some distance from TG 50.3, while the SBDs remained on deck, fully loaded. The VF-9 Hellcats that had managed to take off raced after the 'Vals', being joined in the pursuit by VF-18 from *Bunker Hill* and VF-22 from *Independence*. Land-based VF-17, with its F4U Corsairs, and Hellcat-equipped VF-33 had been patrolling over TG 50.3 at the time, and they joined the melee. In the confused combat that followed, the US Navy pilots claimed 85 Japanese aeroplanes shot down – more than actually participated in the attack. VF-9 claimed 41 aircraft destroyed, while VF-18 claimed 25 and VF-17 claimed 19. Regardless of the precise number shot down, Japanese losses were heavy. The 1st Koku Sentai alone appears to have had 17 of its 'Val' dive-bombers destroyed, as well as all 14 of its 'Kate' torpedo-bombers and two Zero-sens, and it failed to inflict any damage on the American carriers.

When the 'Vals' launched their attack, the VF-9 pilots were joining up to escort the VT-9 Avengers to Rabaul. As the IJN aircraft commenced their dives on the carriers, the fighter directors on *Essex* ordered the Hellcats that had taken off to repel the attack instead. Although the 'Vals' dropped their ordnance before VF-9 could reach them, the Hellcat pilots went after the fleeing dive-bombers as they headed back to Rabaul, with devastating results. The 'Vals' stood little chance against the Hellcats, although in several instances the rear gunners bravely continued firing until they were either killed or their aeroplane crashed into the sea. Most of the VF-9 pilots claimed their 'Vals' in high-side runs from astern – a few good bursts into the fuselage and the unprotected fuel tanks in the wing areas were all that was needed to set a 'Val' on fire.

Lts Jack Onstott and Charles Moutenot and future ace Lt(jg) Albert Martin each claimed two victories in their attacks on the formations. Onstott shot down his pair of 'Vals' in quick succession with stern runs, both Japanese aircraft bursting into flames. These turned out to be his only victories of the war. Martin also shot down a 'Val', flying at only 200 ft, in a stern attack, and then made a head-on pass on a second one flying even lower. He hit it in the engine, which set the 'Val' on fire, and sent it crashing into the sea for the first of his eventual five victory claims. Charles Moutenot made a beam attack on one 'Val' and set it on fire with four bursts. Finding another one flying just above the sea, he came in from the stern and hit it with a long burst that sent the 'Val' gliding down into the sea on fire.

Elsewhere, Lt Cdr Houck had shot down a 'Val' moments after taking off from *Essex*. Having made a left turn at 1400 ft following his launch, Houck saw a 'Val' below him flying at 500 ft. He dropped down quickly, and in a stern attack set the 'Val' on fire, sending it crashing into the water for his first aerial victory of the day. Lts Leslie DeCew and Reuben Denoff and Ens John Franks, all future Hellcat aces, also opened their scoring by shooting down a 'Val' each in this encounter. Lt Mayo Hadden also claimed a 'Val' for his second kill of the war.

The VF-9 pilots broke off their attacks on the few surviving dive-bombers when they received word from the fighter director aboard *Essex* that the ship's radar had detected further approaching formations – 'Kate' torpedo-bombers. The Hellcats were given a vector and the approximate distance of the enemy formations from TG 50.3. As the Hellcats came into range, one VF-9 pilot called out over the radio, 'Jesus Christ, there's millions of them!'

In the attacks that followed the unit claimed 18 'Kates' shot down, with Lt Cdr Houck and Lt(jg) Martin being credited with two apiece – the latter successes making Martin the high scorer of the day. Houck went after a 'Kate' beginning its torpedo run, and in a long stern attack sent the aeroplane crashing into the sea trailing smoke. He then saw a second 'Kate' nearby flying just above the sea, and took a full deflection shot from 500 ft above, apparently without effect. Turning hard, Houck came in from the stern, and after his second short burst the 'Kate' caught fire and crashed.

Martin had a similar experience, making a full deflection shot against a 'Kate', and then swinging around to come in from the rear, firing until his quarry burst into flames and plunged into the sea. Seeing another 'Kate' coming towards him, Martin opened fire in a 45-degree deflection shot, getting hits in the fuselage. He watched as the torpedo-bomber dropped away and hit the water in flames.

Lt Marvin Franger made a high-side run on a 'Kate', hitting the Japanese aircraft hard and causing it to trail smoke. He watched as the IJN pilot tried to turn away from his attacker, only to catch a wing in the sea and crash for Franger's second kill of the war.

Lt(jg) Howard Hudson was another future VF-9 ace who opened his scoring in this action. As he made a stern approach on a 'Kate' its rear gunner opened fire, fortunately without doing any damage. The 'Kate' started smoking, then burst into flames

Lt(jg) William Bonneau claimed a 'Zeke' in the morning strike on Rabaul and a 'Val' and a 'Kate' during the afternoon raid on TG 50.3 for his first victories (*via the author*)

Lt(jg) Eugene Valencia had known Bill Bonneau before they enlisted in the US Navy. After joining VF-9, the pair frequently flew together. Valencia also claimed his first victories on 11 November – a 'Zeke', a 'Val' and 1.5 'Kates' (*via the author*)

as the others had done, before hitting the sea. Lts DeCew and Denoff added to their scores for the day, shooting down a 'Kate' each. Lt(jg) Matthew Byrnes, who would become a Hellcat ace later in the war flying with VBF-12, claimed a 'Kate' and a 'Betty' bomber to add to a 'Zeke' he had downed that morning over Rabaul.

Two of VF-9's sections did particularly well during the defence of TG 50.3. Lt(jg) Burton Bardeen and his wingman, future ace Lt(jg) Edward McGowan, claimed six Japanese aircraft between them. They first caught up with the 'Vals' after their attacks, each claiming one shot down. The dive-bombers were flying as low as 20 ft above the water, trying to escape detection by the marauding Hellcats. Bardeen made a high-side run from the port quarter on his 'Val', closing in for a stern attack as the rear gunner opened fire on him. Raking the fuselage up to the engine, Bardeen set the 'Val' on fire and saw it crash. McGowan also set a 'Val' ablaze in a stern attack, and he saw it crash into the sea.

Sent after the 'Kates' as they began their torpedo runs, Bardeen and McGowan joined up to shoot down one between them. Having seen their victim hit the water, each pilot went after another torpedo-bomber, catching them as they headed for the destroyer screen and setting them on fire. McGowan then saw what he identified as a 'Tony' flying several thousand feet above him. This was more likely to have been a 'Judy' (D4Y1 carrier reconnaissance aircraft), as the Japanese Army Air Force (JAAF) rarely accompanied its IJN counterparts on combat missions. Furthermore, at this time most of the JAAF's Ki-61 units were fighting in New Guinea. McGowan climbed up beneath the 'Judy', apparently unobserved, and fired into its fuselage from below, setting the aeroplane on fire and giving him three and a half victory claims for the day.

Lt(jg)s Bill Bonneau and Eugene Valencia flew again as a section that afternoon and claimed two victories each. Valencia was also credited with an additional half-victory for a 'Kate' he shot down with Lt(jg) George Cohan. Bonneau and Valencia each flamed a 'Val', and were then called off the dive-bombers to go after the approaching 'Kate' formations. Bonneau saw Lt Jack Onstott make a dummy run on a 'Kate', forcing the aeroplane to drop its torpedo. Unknown to Bonneau, only one of Onstott's machine guns was working, so he was unable to shoot it down. Bonneau duly dove after the 'Kate' and made a stern attack, getting hits in the fuselage and wing area with a long burst. A long flame shot out of the aircraft's fuselage and it slowly rolled over onto its back and plunged into the ocean.

Eugene Valencia also made a stern attack on a 'Kate' before it could release its torpedo, sending the aeroplane down into the sea. Finding another target, he began his run from the starboard side just as Lt(jg) Cohan intercepted the same aeroplane. As the two Hellcat pilots pulled up and away after their attack, the 'Kate' crashed into the sea. In their first day of aerial combat, Bonneau and Valencia each claimed a 'Zeke', a 'Val' and a 'Kate' destroyed, with Valencia getting a half-share in a second torpedo-bomber.

The most remarkable kill of the day belonged to VF-9's Lt(jg) George Blair, whose guns would only operate intermittently. He would fire a short burst, only to have the guns jam, preventing him from shooting down any of the 'Vals' under attack. When the 'Kate' formation came in, Blair joined the other Hellcat pilots going after them. He came in on a stern run on a 'Kate' and opened fire, only to have the machine guns jam again after only a short burst. Determined to knock his target down, Blair closed on the 'Kate' and then flew directly over it, at which point he released his drop tank from just 12 ft above the Japanese aeroplane. The drop tank hit the torpedo-bomber, sending it crashing into the sea in flames.

By the end of the day VF-9 had submitted claims for 55 Japanese aircraft shot down over Rabaul and in defence of TG 50.3 – a record for a US Navy fighter squadron that stood until the Marianas Turkey Shoot on 19 June 1944. In all, 23 pilots submitted claims for 'Vals', 'Kates' and other aircraft shot down.

One of VF-9's F6F-3 Hellcats with three victory markings beneath its cockpit. This rare aerial photograph was probably taken soon after the Rabaul strikes (*80G-217620, NARA*)

Eleven pilots were given credit for assists where several of them had been firing on the same enemy aeroplane and believed that their fire had contributed to the aircraft's destruction. Multiple pilots attacking the same target no doubt contributed to the number of claims made exceeding the number of actual Japanese losses.

But regardless of the number of Japanese aircraft destroyed, VF-9 and CAG-9 had contributed to two vitally important achievements by the fast carriers. Firstly, the successful attacks on Rabaul had demonstrated the striking power of multi-carrier task forces, which, when used offensively, could help protect amphibious operations through strikes on nearby Japanese bases. The second achievement was the defence of TG 50.3 from attack by land-based aircraft. The fear that carriers would not be able to stand up to attacks by land-based air forces – a major concern in the interwar years – had been shown not to be true in all cases.

TARAWA AND KWAJALEIN

TG 50.3 briefly returned to Espiritu Santo, then on 14 November 1943 sailed north to rejoin TF 50 for Operation *Galvanic* (the invasion of Tarawa). TF 38 had been re-designated TG 50.4 and sent north as well, giving TF 50 a total of 11 fleet and light carriers in its four task groups.

Arriving near Tarawa on 18 November, TG 50.3 immediately launched the first attacks on the island. CAG-9 sent out five strikes during the day, accompanying aeroplanes from *Bunker Hill* and *Independence*. Lt Cdr Phil Torrey led eight Hellcats on the first strike – a fighter sweep over Tarawa to eliminate any Japanese fighters. The VF-9 pilots found no enemy aircraft in the air, but strafed three aeroplanes on the airfield on Tarawa and made repeated runs against the installations on the field.

On the fourth strike of the day, Lt Cdr Torrey went out again with 12 Hellcats to escort VB-9's SBDs in an attack on nearby Betio Island, going in to strafe anti-aircraft positions before the dive-bombers came in. Returning to *Essex* after the strike, the fighters saw a Mitsubishi F1M Type 0 observation seaplane (codenamed 'Pete' by the Allies) approaching Betio at around 6000 ft. Seeing no one ahead of him going after the 'Pete',

Hamilton McWhorter launched his own attack, coming in for a stern run, only to have the Japanese floatplane do a 'split-S' and dive beneath him. McWhorter manoeuvred to come in on a high-side run from the left, but the 'Pete' again evaded with a hard right turn, diving for a cloud below. McWhorter followed the 'Pete' into the cloud and, seeing a dark image ahead of him, opened fire. Upon diving out of the cloud moments later, McWhorter saw the 'Pete' heading for the sea in flames for his fourth victory.

The next day McWhorter got his fifth kill and became the first Hellcat ace. While flying a CAP in Lt Hadden's division, with Lt(jg) Eugene Valencia as his wingman, McWhorter and his fellow Naval Aviators were ordered by *Essex*'s fighter director to investigate a low-flying 'bogey' around 30 miles from TG 50.3. Closing in, McWhorter spotted a 'Betty' bomber. Seeing the approaching Hellcats, the pilot of the 'Betty' dove down to wave-top height and attempted to escape. Lt Hadden and his wingman, Lt Jack Kitchen, came in from the stern, apparently forgetting the 'Betty's' 20 mm tail gun, which opened fire on the fighters as they approached. McWhorter raced ahead of the 'Betty' to set himself up for a flat side run, thereby avoiding the tail gun. Coming from the right side, McWhorter opened fire, hitting the bomber's centre fuselage and setting its port engine on fire. The Betty crashed into the water and disintegrated, giving McWhorter the distinction of becoming the first VF-9 pilot, and the first Hellcat pilot, to win the coveted title of ace.

Upon McWhorter's return to *Essex*, the maintenance crews found that he had fired only 87 rounds from his six machine guns. Lt Cdr Torrey promptly dubbed him 'One Slug' McWhorter for his parsimonious use of ammunition and excellent shooting.

Later that afternoon Lt Leslie DeCew and his wingman were vectored onto another 'Betty' snooper. DeCew shot it down using similar tactics to those employed by McWhorter, making a beam run to avoid the tail gun, closing to a 30-degree deflection shot and sending the bomber down to explode when it hit the water. These were VF-9's only aerial victories during Operation *Galvanic*.

The invasion began on 20 November, and for the next five days the squadron flew CAS missions for the US Marine Corps fighting to capture Tarawa and CAPs over TG 50.3. The Hellcats flew repeated strafing runs on targets all over the island, going after anti-aircraft guns and reported Japanese positions. Only one aeroplane was lost on these missions, Lt Harold Vita having to ditch when anti-aircraft fire cut his oil line. Vita ditched and got into his dinghy, where he spent the next eight hours until a destroyer from the TG 50.3 rescued him. Tarawa was declared secured on 24 November after the invading forces had incurred heavy casualties.

Leaving *Bunker Hill* and USS *Monterey* (CVL-26) behind in the Gilberts to protect Tarawa and sending TG 50.4 back to Pearl Harbor, Adm Raymond Spruance instructed Rear Adm Pownall to take TG 50.1 (*Yorktown*, *Lexington* and *Cowpens*) and a reorganised TG 50.3 (*Essex*, *Enterprise* and *Belleau Wood*) to strike Kwajalein Atoll, in the Marshall Islands, and destroy Japanese shipping, aircraft and installations there, and to obtain photographic coverage for the invasion planned for January 1944. The IJN had instructed the 281st Kokutai to defend Kwajalein, its 21 A6Ms arriving on the island of Roi, in the northern section of the Atoll, on 3 December – just 24 hours before the American carrier strike.

Approaching Kwajalein from the northeast on the morning of 4 December 1943, the carriers began launching their aircraft a little after 0700 hrs. CAG-9 sent off 24 SBDs from VB-9, 19 TBFs from VT-9 and 22 of VF-9's F6Fs as escorts. Their target was the island of Roi. Once overhead at 13,000 ft, the torpedo-bombers were ordered to attack two Japanese light cruisers in the atoll. The dive-bombers, however, split up, half going against the cruisers and half targeting the airfield on Roi.

Lt Cdr Torrey led his division in on a strafing run on the airfield, shooting up several 'Betty' bombers but failing to set any on fire. Coming off their run, Torrey and his division encountered a 'Zeke' preparing to attack the dive-bombers as they pulled out of their dives. Torrey and the other pilots attacked the 'Zeke', but only managed to damage it.

The airfield on Roi Island under attack on 29 January 1944, with Japanese aeroplanes burning on the runway (*80G-216620, NARA*)

Lt(jg) Albert Martin was flying as section leader with Lt(jg) George Blair as his wingman, escorting an SBD taking photographs of the attack. There were eight to ten 'Zekes' flying in the area, and four came in to make runs on the photo-aeroplane. As one attacked head-on at 1500 ft, Martin came in at a 45-degree angle on the 'Zeke', forcing it to make a 'split-S' manoeuvre in order to get away. Blair immediately went after the 'Zeke', attacking it from above and to the rear and getting good hits in the fuselage. Moments later the fighter made contact with the water and exploded. Finding a second 'Zeke' coming in low over the sea, Blair dived on the Japanese fighter, which turned sharply to the left in an attempt to escape the Hellcat. Blair pressed home his attack to the point where his Japanese opponent misjudged his altitude and crashed into the sea. This gave Blair the unusual distinction of having shot down one Japanese aircraft, destroyed another with his drop tank and manoeuvred a third into the water.

Meanwhile, Martin had gone after another 'Zeke' that he spotted making a run on one of the escorting Hellcats. He quickly shot it down, making him VF-9's second ace.

During the course of these early clashes between the F6F and the A6M, Naval Aviators from VF-9 had noted that at higher speeds of 200 knots (230 mph) or above at low altitudes, a Hellcat could match a 'Zeke' turn for turn if the pilot used his combat flaps.

The attacks on Kwajalein were not as effective as they could have been, particularly against the 'Betty' bombers lined up on the airfield at Roi, but Rear Adm Pownall refused a request to launch a second strike and ordered the force to retire. *Essex* reached Pearl Harbor on 9 December 1943. For the next five weeks VF-9 and the rest of CAG-9 conducted training exercises, interspersed with spending five days at a rest home on Waikiki Beach that a private individual had offered the use of to the US Navy.

The first stay began with what the VF-9 war diary recorded as 'a five-day binge. The day started with milk punch for breakfast for those who could, followed by beer until the heavy liquor came out in the afternoon'. After an evening of dancing, the pilots went to bed 'more or less plastered, only to wake the next morning for the same routine'. After another exuberant celebration, VF-9's Medical Officer brought a ten-foot palm tree, 'borrowed' from a local yacht club, on board *Essex* and placed it in the squadron ready room on the pretext that it was to be used in medical experiments!

While training and resting at Pearl Harbor, there were several changes in command. Toward the end of December the acting CO of CAG-9, Lt Cdr Paul Emrick, was re-assigned away from *Essex*. Lt Cdr Phil Torrey was promoted to take over command of the Carrier Air Group in his place, with Lt Cdr Herbert Houck being promoted to lead VF-9.

On 16 January 1944 *Essex* left Pearl Harbor to participate in the invasion of Kwajalein (Operation *Flintlock*) as part of a renamed TF 58, now the Fast Carrier Task Force, under the command of Rear Adm Marc Mitscher. *Essex* now made up part of TG 58.2, with USS *Intrepid* (CV-11) and the newly arrived USS *Cabot* (CVL-28). The invasion plan called for the capture of the islands of Roi and Namur, in the northern part of Kwajalein Atoll, and the island of Kwajalein itself in the south. With the latter in American hands, the remaining Japanese garrisons in the Marshall Islands could be neutralised. Kwajalein and the nearby Majuro Atoll would serve as stepping-stones for the western march across the Central Pacific.

The 12 carriers of TF 58 were to launch strikes on both objectives on 29-30 January – just before the landings on 1 February – to destroy any Japanese aircraft and to establish air superiority over the area. TG 58.2 was assigned the task of attacking military installations on Roi and Namur before the Fourth Marine Division landings on the islands. Once the troops were ashore, the Carrier Air Groups were to provide CAS for them until Roi and Namur were secured. Unbeknown to the US Navy, the IJN had decided not to reinforce their garrisons in the Marshalls or contest an invasion with a fleet action. The 281st Kokutai was on its own.

On 29 January *Essex* began launching the first strike of the day before dawn so as to arrive over Roi a little before sunrise. CAG-9 sent out 19 Hellcats from VF-9 and six of VT-9's Avengers. The F6F pilots were to clear the air of any Japanese fighters and destroy any aeroplanes on the airfield at Roi before the torpedo- and dive-bombers came in. Lt Cdr Houck led his five divisions to the target at low altitude, climbing to 6000 ft for the final run in. Approaching Roi, the pilots could see ten to fifteen enemy fighters flying over the island. The pilots estimated that there were around 20 twin-engine aeroplanes and 30 to 35 single-engined machines on the airfield. Each of the Hellcat pilots had been assigned a single revetment for the first strafing run, concentrating on the single-engined fighters.

Lt(jg) Hamilton McWhorter was leading a section in Lt Mayo Hadden's division, with Lt(jg) Bill Gehoe as his wingman. Coming in on Roi, the pilots found a layer of thin cloud covering the area. To maintain surprise, Hadden led his division up into the clouds, the pilots spreading out as they entered the overcast.

Hamilton McWhorter shows one of *Essex*'s Landing Signal Officers how he shot down two 'Hamps' over Roi, catching one IJN fighter before the Hellcats began their strafing run over the island and getting a second after climbing away and finding a Japanese machine directly ahead of him (*80G-217500, NARA*)

35

After a short period, when Hadden calculated that they were close to Roi, he ordered the division to dive out of the clouds and begin their strafing runs. For some reason McWhorter hesitated slightly. When he came out of the clouds he found himself about a half a mile behind his division. Racing to catch up, he saw a 'Hamp' (Mitsubishi A6M3 Type 0 Fighter) above and behind the rest of the division, preparing to attack. Concentrating on the three Hellcats ahead of him, the 'Hamp' pilot did not see McWhorter, who closed rapidly from astern. The Hellcat pilot fired one long burst, hitting the 'Hamp' in the fuselage. The Japanese fighter erupted in flames and fell into the sea below.

A VF-9 pilot waits in the cockpit while his Hellcat gets re-armed and refuelled for the next strike on Roi (*80G-217498, NARA*)

As the Hellcat pilots entered their dives to strafe the airfield, anti-aircraft and machine gun fire rose up to meet them. The Hellcats went in fast, at 300-320 knots, and manoeuvred violently on their recovery, trying to align their runs so as to avoid concentrations of anti-aircraft batteries. Most of the pilots made six passes over the airfield, strafing single- and twin-engined aeroplanes. Not all the Japanese aircraft on the field burned, however, so it was difficult to determine exactly how much damage had been done. Nevertheless, the pilots believed that they had destroyed between 15 and 18 'Betty' bombers belonging to the 752nd and 753rd Kokutai, as well as other twin-engined types, and between 22 and 24 single-engined fighters. This attack effectively wiped out the 281st Kokutai, which lost 25 Zero-sens destroyed on the ground on this day and the next.

The A6Ms that had managed to get aloft before Roi was targeted tried to disrupt the strafing attacks, but they enjoyed little success. During one strafing run Lt(jg) Marvin Franger saw a 'Hamp' manoeuvring to get on the tail of another Hellcat about 1000 ft ahead of him. The F6F pilot evaded the 'Zeke' with a high-speed turn to the left, which his opponent did not follow. Instead, the IJN pilot began a barrel roll, apparently intent on coming down behind Franger. The latter executed a sharp pull-up and fired a burst into the 'Hamp' when the fighter was on its back at the top of its roll. Franger must have killed the pilot as the 'Hamp' completed its roll and went straight down into the sea.

A few moments later another Zero-sen made a beam attack on Franger, manoeuvring to get on his tail. Franger made a high-speed turn to the left. Instead of following, the 'Zeke' pilot turned to the right to go after Franger's wingman. Franger completed his turn and came at the 'Zeke' head on, getting hits in the engine and wing root area that set the aircraft's fuel tanks alight and sent it spinning down into the sea.

As Lt(jg) Eugene Valencia and his division leader, Lt Moutenot, climbed away from one of their strafing runs they saw two Japanese fighters that they identified as JAAF 'Oscars' (although they were almost certainly 'Hamps') attacking several Hellcats completing their strafing runs. Moutenot made a run on one of the fighters, which immediately pulled up into a loop to avoid his fire. Valencia followed his opponent through the loop and got in a no-deflection shot from directly astern. The fighter blew up under his fire.

With the Hellcats making repeated strafing runs, the Zero-sens that tried to intervene were continually at risk from F6Fs coming in behind them. Indeed, Lt Leslie DeCew shot down a 'Zeke' that flew directly in front of him just as he was beginning his strafing pass on the airfield. Having apparently missed with his first burst of fire from directly astern, DeCew watched as the 'Zeke' attempted to dive away. His second burst was a deflection shot, fired as he dove on the 'Zeke' as it attempted to escape. DeCew finally hit the Japanese fighter directly from behind with his third burst, sending it down smoking to explode in flames when it hit the water.

Lt(jg) Stephen Wright was also seen to destroy a 'Zeke', but on a later strafing run anti-aircraft fire hit his Hellcat and he pulled off the target with his aeroplane smoking. Wright headed out to the open ocean, where he bailed out. An OS2U sent to the area failed to find him, and the Naval Aviator was listed as missing in action.

Other Hellcats from VF-6, VF-10 and VF-31 added to the destruction of Japanese aircraft in the air and on the ground. The 281st Kokutai had been so badly devastated by the opening attack on Roi that during the next strike flown later that same day, which saw 11 TBFs from VT-9 escorted by VF-9, the Hellcat pilots encountered just one solitary Zero-sen. VF-9 flew a total of five strikes on Roi on 29 January, continuing to strafe the aircraft and installations on the airfield and maintaining CAPs over the area so that the dive- and torpedo-bombers could do their work unmolested.

On the last mission of the day Lt(jg) Louis Menard came off his strafing run to find a 'Kate' flying low to the southwest of Roi, probably having taken off from another Japanese air base on a nearby atoll without knowledge of the attacks on the island. The unfortunate 'Kate' stood little chance. Menard did a wing over and came in on the torpedo-bomber's tail, at which point he fired a long burst that hit the fuselage and wing areas. The 'Kate' fell into the sea in a mass of flames.

Lt(jg) Marvin Franger (right) describes how he shot down a 'Hamp' over Roi, pulling up to fire at the Japanese fighter as it was at the top of a roll. Franger managed to shoot down another fighter a short time later. These were his third and fourth victories (*80G-217501, NARA*)

The strikes and CAPs continued on 30 January – the day before the landing. With no Japanese air opposition, VF-9's pilots spent most of their time performing repeated strafing attacks on Roi and nearby Namur Island, sometimes dropping their belly tanks to start fires. On the day of the invasion, VF-9 flew more CAPs over the invasion fleet and several strafing missions in support of the landings. The CAPs continued until 3 February, with the loss of one pilot, Lt(jg) John Benton, who had crashed and was killed shortly after taking off on 1 February.

Over the five days of operations in support of the invasion, VF-9 had claimed nine Japanese aircraft shot down and 25 twin-engined and 30 single-engined machines destroyed on the ground. With the island secure, the main carrier force withdrew. Leaving TG 58.4 to cover the invasion fleet for the capture of Eniwetok, the rest of TF 58 returned to the newly-captured anchorage at Majuro, where VF-9 received replacement aeroplanes and five replacement pilots drawn from VF-16 and VF-36. A rumour went around that CAG-9 was about to be relieved, but when *Essex* was re-supplied with ammunition, the pilots realised another operation would soon be upon them. On 12 February 1944 *Essex* sailed out of Majuro as part of TG 58.2, destination unknown.

TRUK

As Cdr Phil Torrey related to a reporter after the attack, 'they didn't tell us where we were going until we were well on the way. They announced our destination over the loudspeaker. It was Truk. My first instinct was to jump overboard'. When Capt Ralph Ofstie, captain of *Essex*, announced that CAG-9 'would be privileged to hit Truk', no doubt other pilots shared Torrey's misgivings.

Truk lagoon was an enigma. The Japanese had taken it over from Germany at the end of World War 1 under a League of Nations mandate. For years, no westerners had been allowed on the islands, which the Japanese had turned into a naval base. Truk was the most important Japanese base in the Central Pacific, having the best anchorage for naval and transport ships, storage and repair depots, a seaplane base and three airfields on the islands in the Truk lagoon. The islands were an important staging post for aeroplanes flying south to Rabaul and on to Japanese bases in the Central Pacific. Truk was known as the 'Gibraltar of the Pacific', a seemingly impregnable outpost that the men on the carriers approached with no little trepidation.

The first American photographic coverage of Truk had only taken place on 4 February 1944, revealing the ships of the IJN's Combined Fleet. The American reconnaissance sortie prompted the withdrawal of the Combined Fleet to avoid attack, leaving only two light cruisers and eight destroyers in Truk lagoon. But rough weather had forced around 50 transports and auxiliary ships to remain at Truk too, while a large number of aeroplanes en route to Rabaul sat on the airfields at Moen, Eten and Param Islands within the lagoon waiting for ferry pilots to take them south.

Several fighter units were also based at Truk in mid-February. The 204th Kokutai and the 504th Kokutai had both been withdrawn from Rabaul back to Truk, while elements of the 201st Kokutai had been moved to Truk from Saipan. The 902nd Kokutai, a fighter and reconnaissance floatplane unit, was also based at Truk with Nakajima Type 2 A6M2-N

A VF-9 Hellcat takes off for the first strike on Truk early on 17 February 1944 (*80G-217587, NARA*)

Japanese shipping comes under attack in Truk lagoon. Hellcats from TF 58 followed the SBDs down in their dives, strafing the ships immediately after the dive-bombers had dropped their ordnance (*80G-215151, NARA*)

floatplane fighters ('Rufes'), F1M2 Type 0 observation seaplanes ('Petes') and Aichi E13A Type 0 reconnaissance seaplanes ('Jakes'). Truk was also the base for several medium bomber and patrol aeroplane Kokutai. In total, the IJN had around 365 aircraft of various types at Truk on the day the US Navy carriers launched their attack on the islands.

TF 58 approached Truk from the northeast early on 17 February 1944, reaching the launch point some 90 miles away from the islands undetected (the After Action Reports list this as 16 February 1944, as the US Navy was following Greenwich Civil Time and did not account for TF 58 having crossed the International Date Line). TF 58's objective was to destroy as many ships and aircraft as possible, and to damage shore installations in two days of continuous strikes. Adm Mitscher planned to begin the strike on Truk with a fighter sweep at dawn by 72 Hellcats whose task it was to clear the skies of Japanese fighters before sending in the dive- and torpedo-bombers against enemy shipping. VF-9 was assigned the task of providing medium altitude cover for other Hellcat squadrons going in to strafe the airfield on Eten Island and the seaplane base on Dublon Island, with a secondary mission of strafing the airfields on Param and Moen islands.

Taking off at 0642 hrs, Lt Cdr Herbert Houck led ten Hellcats aloft, with Lt(jg)s Howard Hudson, Louis Menard and Matthew Byrnes in his division. Lt Jack Kitchen led the second division, with Ens John Franks and Lt(jg)s Marvin Franger and Henry Schiebler. Lt Charles Moutenot led the third division (consisting of only three F6Fs), with Lt(jg)s Bill Bonneau and Eugene Valencia. Houck led the formation towards Truk at a height of 1000 ft. When they were about 15 minutes away, he took his men up to 14,000 ft – their assigned patrol altitude. As they approached the target area, the divisions were spread out, flying about a mile apart. Because of the distance between them, the first and second divisions did not see Moutenot's division come under attack a short while later.

Coming in toward Truk lagoon, one of the three pilots in Moutenot's division saw a small group of fighters above him, but from the light colouring on the underside of their fuselages and wings he assumed that these were other Hellcats assigned to high cover. A few minutes later six to eight 'Zekes' jumped the division. Moutenot, Bonneau and Valencia did not realise they were under attack until the Japanese pilots opened fire on them in overhead runs. The three pilots instinctively broke away in violent evasive manoeuvres to avoid their attackers. With no chance to join back up, they ended up fighting their own individual defensive battles. Moutenot entered a steep, high-speed dive to get away, recovering above the sea. Climbing back up to altitude, he looked for friendly fighters, but immediately came under attack again and had to dive away to escape. This happened to him 12 times whilst over the target area.

He claimed one 'Zeke' shot down in flames and hit another 'Zeke' that he claimed as probably destroyed.

For Bill Bonneau, this first fighter sweep over Truk was his most harrowing combat experience in World War 2;

'We were jumped and I got separated, and every aeroplane I saw had a big red dot on its side. After one knocked my hydraulic system out, I got rid of them by using the Navy's oldest technical manoeuvre – "Get the Hell out of there".'

When first attacked Bonneau went into a tight left turn, reversing direction as his attacker flew past him. He made a series of turns with the 'Zeke', getting in several bursts as the two fighters descended from 12,000 ft down to 6000 ft, where the enemy machine went into a tight spiral down into the sea. Bonneau continued to fly around the area on his own for the next ten minutes. Seeing six 'Rufes' above him, he climbed up behind the last floatplane in the formation and opened fire. The 'Rufe' streamed black smoke and spun down into the water. The remaining five floatplane fighters turned on him, hitting his Hellcat with 7.7 mm fire, but Bonneau manoeuvred away in a sharp climbing turn and came back to launch a high-side run on one of the 'Rufes'. He got a good burst into the fuselage and the aircraft blew up. While he was attacking the 'Rufe', a 'Zeke' latched onto Bonneau's tail, forcing him to dive away from 12,000 ft down to 2000 ft.

With his aeroplane damaged, Bonneau decided to head back to *Essex* alone. Heading out he came across two more 'Rufes' some 15 miles from Truk lagoon. He made a high-side run on the lead floatplane, setting it on fire and watching the pilot bail out. These four victories made Bonneau an ace.

Eugene Valencia also became an ace that day, shooting down three 'Zekes', but the mission was formative in another way. His experiences over Truk that morning stimulated his thinking about aerial combat tactics, giving him ideas that he would later perfect in training and utilise during his next combat tour with great effect.

Like Charles Moutenot, Valencia entered a steep dive as soon as he was attacked, but pulling out low over the water he found himself bracketed by six to eight 'Zekes' – most likely the same group that had attacked the division. Valencia chose to continue to fly straight and level, deciding that in an evasive turning fight the 'Zekes' would have the advantage. Two 'Zekes' made high-side runs on him, but only managed to get a few hits with their 7.7mm machine guns. On the third run against him, two 'Zekes' made the mistake of pulling up in front of Valencia, who immediately opened fire on the lead fighter and shot it down in flames. He quickly fired at the second 'Zeke' and saw it explode. Two more 'Zekes' came at him from the left, and as they turned in on their attack Valencia

Lt Cdr Herbert Houck led his division down to strafe the seaplane base on Moen Island, in Truk lagoon, which can be seen here burning at the bottom of the photograph. The seaplane base on Dublon Island was also attacked, its location being pinpointed by the smoke in the centre background (*80G-216898, NARA*)

Lt(jg) Louis Menard (standing in hatchway) describes to fellow VF-9 pilots how he shot down four Japanese aircraft over Truk, thus becoming an ace. Menard was, like Marvin Franger, one of the few US Navy pilots to claim victories on three combat tours and to have kills against more than one Axis air force. Like several other VF-9 pilots, he went on to fly with VBF-12, claiming one last victory during the strikes on Tokyo in February 1945 (*80G-217574, NARA*)

turned in on them to get in a head-on pass. He hit the lead 'Zeke' which burst into flames and crashed into the sea, giving Valencia a chance to escape. These were Valencia's fifth, sixth and seventh victories, making him an ace.

During these combats Valencia noticed that the Japanese pilots did not seem to know how to react when he responded aggressively to their attacks. 'I discovered at Truk that once you take the offensive the Jap doesn't know what to do', he later commented. He realised through this experience that this flaw in Japanese fighter tactics was something that could be exploited. On his return from this first mission to Truk, Valencia famously said, 'Those Grummans are beautiful aeroplanes. If they could cook I'd marry one'.

While Moutenot, Bonneau and Valencia were fighting individually for their survival, the remaining two VF-9 divisions continued into the target area. Herbert Houck led his division in two circuits over the target area. Seeing that there were numerous dogfights going on over Truk lagoon that were keeping the Japanese fighters occupied, and more IJN aircraft could be seen taking off from the airfields, Houck decided to take his division down in strafing attacks on their assigned targets – the seaplane base on Moen Island and the airfield at Param Island. Houck led his pilots in five strafing runs against the seaplane base, setting ten to twelve aeroplanes on fire and damaging others. Moving on to the Param airfield, the pilots made five runs against an estimated 20 to 25 aeroplanes ('Bettys' and 'Kates'), leaving around 15 of them on fire.

During the strafing runs 'Petes' and 'Kates' continued to take off in an attempt to escape the attacks. Whilst over Moen Houck pulled up to find a 'Pete' ahead of him, which he quickly shot down. As he came in on a strafing run Louis Menard saw a 'Pete' ahead of him, so he went after it. Just as he came in range the 'Pete' dived into a small cloud. Menard fired into the cloud anyway, and to his surprise the 'Pete' exploded – both crewmen bailed out. These two kills made Menard an ace. Matthew Byrnes also claimed a 'Pete' over Moen. Over Param airfield Houck again found a Japanese aeroplane ahead of him as he pulled up from his strafing run. A 'Kate' had just taken off, and it was at 200 ft when Houck came in from behind and shot it down for his fifth kill. Louis Menard caught two 'Kates' taking off from Param during his strafing runs, shooting both down for his third and fourth kills of the day. Henry Hudson also saw a 'Kate' flying low over the water and sent it crashing into the sea for his second victory.

Jack Kitchen's division ran into Japanese fighters soon after Moutenot's division had come under attack. The pilots estimated that there were around 50 Japanese aircraft in the air, with more taking off. The division engaged several groups of 'Zekes' over the lagoon in a fight that turned into a general melee. As had happened to Moutenot's division, Kitchen and his pilots soon split up because they were forced to take violent evasive action. The presence of cloud in the target area assisted them in their fight against overwhelming odds, the four Hellcat pilots individually engaging enemy fighters for 30 minutes.

Kitchen shot down a 'Rufe' in a head-on run, his burst of fire hitting the engine and setting the floatplane alight. He then engaged a 'Zeke', getting good hits that sent it down in a steep dive – he claimed this latter success as a probable. Kitchen's wingman, John Franks, saw a 'Zeke' coming in on his tail in a high-side run. Franks went into a dive to pick up speed and then pulled up, at the same time dropping his flaps. As the 'Zeke' overshot him, Franks turned inside the fighter and opened fire in a no-deflection shot. The A6M exploded. Encountering a 'Pete' flying above the melee, Franks set this aeroplane on fire and saw the crew bail out. He then attacked a 'Zeke' from head on as it pulled out of a run against two Hellcats. Franks set the fighter on fire and saw the pilot bail out. This gave him a total of four victories, and he would have to wait until February 1945 to become an ace.

Marvin Franger also shot down a 'Zeke' in a head-on run for his fifth victory. As he recalled later;

'Right over the centre of Truk all hell broke loose. That was the most scared I ever was. I was doing everything in the book. After I shook one I climbed a little, dodging AA fire, when another one came up beneath me. I rolled over and he pulled up in a nearly vertical climb. He was coming straight up and I was going straight down. He was firing and I was firing, but I hit him first. He burst into flames as we went by each other.'

At some point while taking evasive action Franger lost his wingman, Lt(jg) Henry Schiebler, who did not return from the mission – no one saw what happened to him. A Japanese fighter may well have shot Schiebler down, although Franger did see an F6F mistakenly make a run on another Hellcat flying behind him, setting the fighter on fire, but Franger could not confirm whether or not this was Schiebler's aeroplane.

On this first sweep VF-9 pilots claimed 21 Japanese aircraft shot down. The other Hellcat squadrons involved in the mission claimed a further 48.

About 30 minutes after the fighter sweep set off, VF-9 began escorting the dive- and torpedo-bombers of VB-9 and VT-9 to Truk to attack shipping. The first escort mission found no enemy fighters, and instead went down to strafe aeroplanes on the airfields. Lt Cdr Phil Torrey led 14 Hellcats on the second escort mission, and this flight did encounter several groups of Japanese fighters. Torrey had Lt(jg) Philip Ball as his wingman, with Lt A B 'Chick' Smith and Lt(jg) William Blackwell completing his division. Lt Mayo Hadden led the second division, with Ens Matthews as his wingman, and Lt(jg)s Hamilton McWhorter and William Gehoe making up the second section. Lt(jg) Albert Martin led the third division, with Lt Reuben Denoff and Lt(jg) James Toliver making up a fourth.

The Hellcats escorted the bombers into Truk lagoon and followed the SBDs down in their dives. As they pulled out, Lt Cdr Torrey led Lt(jg) Ball in a strafing attack on the airfield at Param Island, adding to the destruction of aeroplanes on the ground.

As 'Chick' Smith was about to push over into a dive to follow the SBDs down, a single 'Zeke' attacked his formation, but fortunately missed him.

A 'Zeke' comes under attack during one of the fierce dogfights over Truk lagoon, the fighter's predicament being captured by the gun camera carried by its opponent. During the hours of daylight on 17 February 1944 US Navy Hellcat pilots claimed more than 80 'Zekes' shot down over Truk (*80G-476109, NARA*)

Lt(jg) Marvin Franger also became an ace over Truk when he claimed a 'Zeke' destroyed. Franger was one of the few US Navy pilots to achieve kills on three combat tours during World War 2, and one of an equally small number to claim victories against more than one Axis air force (*via the author*)

Lt Armistead B Smith was one of the VF-9 pilots who became an ace over Truk, claiming three 'Zekes' destroyed. Five days later he shot down a 'Betty' for his sixth, and last, kill with VF-9. Smith went on to claim four more victories flying F6F-5 Hellcats with VBF-12 during the Okinawa campaign of 1945 (*via the author*)

Seeing tracers passing over his aeroplane, Smith chopped his throttle and put his F6F into a skid to make the 'Zeke' overrun him. As the latter sailed past, Smith pulled up into a steep climb, having no difficulty in following the lighter Japanese fighter. Smith hit the 'Zeke's' port wing and set it on fire, the aeroplane spinning down into the water. Some minutes later, while flying near Moen Island, Smith saw two 'Zekes' taking off from the airfield at the northern end of the island. Diving down on them, he hit one of them so hard that it exploded in front of him. Smith also scored enough hits on the second machine to send it spinning into the water. These three kills made him an ace. On his way back to *Essex* he ran out of fuel and had to ditch, although Smith was quickly picked up by a destroyer.

Just before the dive-bombers started their attack, Mayo Hadden's division ran into a formation of around 15 'Zekes' and 'Hamps', with one group at 10,000 ft and a second at 3000 ft. Hamilton McWhorter and his wingman Bud Gehoe took on three 'Zekes' off to the left of the formation of dive-bombers they were escorting at 10,000 ft. McWhorter and Gehoe turned into them. 'They fought as though they were in a daze'. McWhorter reported. 'My wingman and I ran into three 'Zekes'. The first had a perfect bead on me, but for some reason or other he didn't fire, and Bud knocked him down. The other two ran right into my sights, one after the other, inside ten seconds and went down. Less than a mile away another Zero [later identified as a "Hamp"] was bearing down on me. He could have got me, but, strangely, he didn't fire either. I let him have a burst and set him afire. He bailed out'. These three victories brought McWhorter's score to ten, making him the first Hellcat double ace of the war.

Mayo Hadden and Ens Matthews, his wingman, had gone down with a section of the dive-bombers. Pulling up after a strafing run, Hadden spotted a 'Zeke' coming in from the right and turned into him. Seeing the Hellcats coming at him, the 'Zeke' pilot pulled up into a nearby cloud.

Hadden and his wingman followed him and caught the 'Zeke' as it came out. The enemy pilot pulled up in a loop, but Hadden was able to follow and got in a good burst as the 'Zeke' reached the top of his loop. Undeterred, the A6M pilot fell off his loop and attempted to come in behind the Hellcats. Hadden manoeuvred with the 'Zeke' and his next burst set it on fire. Pulling up above a nearby cloud formation, Hadden found another 'Zeke' and attacked, getting hits in the fuselage area. The fighter dove straight down into the water. Continuing to cover the same area, Hadden came across a third 'Zeke' and once again scored hits in the vulnerable fuselage area. The 'Zeke' dove away, and as it went down it started to burn. Moments later the fighter crashed into Truk lagoon. These three kills made Hadden an ace – he had become the seventh VF-9 pilot to achieve acedom on 17 February.

CAG-9 flew four more strikes on Truk that day, but VF-9 pilots had only one more encounter with Japanese aircraft when Lt(jg) George Cohan shot at a 'Rufe' and claimed it as a probable. With no aerial opposition, the fighters went down with the dive- and torpedo-bombers to strafe shipping in the lagoon and any remaining aircraft on the airfields.

This pattern continued the next day, 18 February. A fighter sweep over Truk first thing in the morning failed to encounter any Japanese aircraft, the IJN's fighter units

Lt Cdr Phil Torrey briefs VF-9 pilots in the ready room aboard CV-9. Lt Cdr Herbert Houck sits in the front row, centre, with Louis Menard just behind him. Hamilton McWhorter sits four rows back on the left, just in front of the Naval Aviator with his hand to his ear (*80G-333202, NARA*)

having suffered heavily in the previous day's fighting. Among the fighter units, the 204th Kokutai lost 18 pilots killed in action, the 501st Kokutai lost 11 Zero-sens and the 902nd Kokutai lost eight of its A6M2-N floatplane fighters.

Finding no aerial opposition after circling over the islands for 20 minutes, the fighters went down to strafe shipping in the lagoon. On the last run, anti-aircraft fire hit Lt(jg) George Blair's fighter and he made a forced landing in the southeast corner of the lagoon. His fellow pilots flew over him protectively, repeatedly strafing a Japanese destroyer that came out to investigate and forcing it away. Lt(jg) Denver Baxter, flying an OS2U Kingfisher from USS *Baltimore* (CA-68) on rescue standby, bravely flew into the lagoon with an escort of two Hellcats and retrieved Blair. He then flew him back to the cruiser. With the Kingfisher back on board, its maintenance

Lt(jg) George Blair, left, with his rescuers, Lt(jg) D F Baxter and Aviation Chief Radioman R F Hickman, who flew into Truk lagoon to rescue Blair after anti-aircraft fire hit his Hellcat, forcing him to ditch (*80G-216624, NARA*)

Louis Menard (looking at the camera) and Hamilton McWhorter (far right) watch as more Japanese flags are added to the VF-9 scoreboard after the successful raids on Truk (*80G-217585, NARA*)

crew found that the floatplane had only a pint of gasoline left in its tanks.

Lt Cdr Torrey led the second, and last, CAG-9 strike of the day. Two Hellcat divisions strafed shipping as they escorted SBDs out of the lagoon, while two fighters strafed single-engined aeroplanes on the airfield at Eten Island (setting five on fire) before CAG-9 retired. TF 58 withdrew that afternoon. The following day American forces landed on Eniwetok without any Japanese aerial opposition.

The strike on Truk had been a resounding success. TF 58's aeroplanes had destroyed an estimated 250 IJN aircraft in the air and on the ground and sunk around 200,000 tons of enemy shipping, including six tankers and 17 transport vessels the Japanese could ill afford to lose, for the loss of 17 carrier aeroplanes. VF-9 claimed 35 aircraft shot down and a further 27 destroyed on the ground in strafing attacks. In the aerial battles over Truk lagoon, seven VF-9 pilots became aces. The fighting confirmed the superiority, if not dominance, of the Hellcat over the Zero-sen. Four VF-9 pilots – Mayo Hadden, Hamilton McWhorter, 'Chick' Smith and Eugene Valencia – returned from Truk claiming three Zero-sens each. The squadron's After Action Reports speak repeatedly of the Hellcat's ability to climb and turn on 'reasonably favourable terms' with a Zero-sen at medium altitudes and speeds over 200 knots. And the Zero-sens proved consistently vulnerable to hits in the wing root or fuselage, a burst of fire quickly setting one on fire.

SAIPAN AND HOME

Instead of returning to the new fleet anchorage at Majuro following the neutralising of Truk, Adm Mitscher took two of his task groups further west to strike at the Marianas. *Essex* was part of a reorganised TG 58.2, with *Yorktown* replacing *Intrepid*, which had been damaged in a Japanese torpedo attack off Truk. TG 58.2 was assigned targets on Guam and Saipan while TG 58.3 covered the islands of Tinian and Rota. Mitscher again planned to begin the attack with an early morning fighter sweep. Once any aerial opposition over the islands had been cleared away, the dive- and torpedo-bombers would go in to strike at airfields and shipping.

After refuelling at sea, the two Task Groups approached the Marianas and came under night torpedo attacks, which the force successfully evaded. At 0834 hrs on 22 February 1944, some 120 miles from Saipan, *Essex* launched ten Hellcats (two divisions and a single section) as part of a fighter sweep, with Lt Cdr Houck leading.

Houck came in over Saipan at 18,000 ft and circled over the airfield for 20 minutes without seeing any enemy aircraft. He then led the formation down to circle at 8000 ft. Seeing undamaged aeroplanes on the airfield below, Houck ordered Lt Mayo Hadden and his wingman, Lt(jg) George Cohan, and Lt(jg) Marvin Franger and his wingman, Ens John Franks, to remain above as cover, while he and five other pilots went down to strafe the aircraft. Houck and the others made several high-speed runs over the airfield, setting five or six twin-engined aeroplanes on fire. Shortly thereafter, more VF-9 Hellcats that were escorting the first bomber strike joined in. Houck then led his formation to the seaplane base on the island, where they set fire to another four or five floatplanes and flying boats before heading back to *Essex*.

Flying cover above, Hadden, Cohan, Franger and Franks ran into a formation of Zero-sens that had apparently taken off from Tinian to intercept the American raid. As the After Action Report recorded;

The airfield on Saipan under attack on 22 February 1944 – VF-9's last action of its second combat cruise (*80G-216627, NARA*)

'Enemy VF pilots encountered in this action appeared to be outstandingly stupid and poorly trained in VF tactics. Evasive manoeuvres on part of "Zeke" pilots almost nil. One "Zeke" pilot attempted to slug it out with an F6F by making a head-on run. "Zeke" came out second best.'

Mayo Hadden repeated his Truk feat of shooting down three 'Zekes' on a single mission. He was flying at 6000 ft when he noticed a fighter beginning to make a high-side run on a formation of Hellcats ahead of him. As the 'Zeke' pulled up from an unsuccessful pass, he flew directly in front of Hadden, who fired as the IJN pilot continued his climb. He scored hits in the fuselage, causing the 'Zeke' to roll over and dive straight down onto Saipan. Hadden saw another 'Zeke' making an approach on some Hellcats so he dove down on it. The IJN pilot turned into Hadden in a head-on run, but the Hellcat's superior firepower won out. The 'Zeke' burst into flames and then exploded, although its pilot somehow managed to bail out.

By now separated from his wingman, Lt(jg) Cohan, Hadden looked around for other Hellcats to join up with and saw two flying below him. As he went down towards them, he saw a third 'Zeke' heading back to Tinian. Diving at high speed on his unsuspecting foe, Hadden opened fire with a long burst that hit the 'Zeke's' fuselage. The fighter began smoking and subsequently lost height and crashed into the sea off Saipan.

Cohan, meanwhile, had come under attack from two 'Zekes' while he was covering Hadden's first attack. He chopped his throttle and threw his aeroplane into a violent skid in order to turn into the attacking 'Zekes', who flew directly under him. Now going onto the offensive, Cohan continued his turn and then made a stern attack on the aircraft that, moments before, had been pursuing him. As he closed on the 'Zekes' he found that one of them was flying just above the other one. He opened fire on the lower 'Zeke', which burst into flames. Keeping his gun button depressed, he then pulled his Hellcat up and aimed at the top 'Zeke', which also burst into flames. A short while later, he found another Zeke and shot it down with a high-side run. Cohan narrowly missed becoming an ace, however, these three victories taking his wartime total to 4.5.

Lt Cdr Phil Torrey, CAG-9 CO, poses with his squadron commanders. These Naval Aviators are, from left to right, Torrey, Lt Cdr Arthur Decker (VB-9), Lt Cdr Donald White (VT-9) and Lt Cdr Herbert Houck (VF-9) (*80G-216633, NARA*)

At the end of the second combat cruise the pilots of VF-9 pose with their scoreboard, which shows victory symbols for six Vichy French and 120 Japanese aeroplanes shot down (*80G-300826, NARA*)

Flying as wingman to Marvin Franger, John Franks saw a 'Zeke' making a run on his section leader. Its pilot, apparently, had not noticed Franks, who was flying slightly behind Franger. He got in a good burst with 30 per cent deflection, leaving the 'Zeke' trailing smoke. It soon fell away in a spin, disappearing into the clouds below. Although Franks could not follow the 'Zeke' down, other pilots saw two A6Ms dive out of the clouds at the time of this encounter and crash, so he was given credit for one of them. This was Franks' all-important fifth kill, making him an ace. Marvin Franger had also enjoyed success during this clash, shooting down a 'Zeke' that had attempted to attack VF-9's high cover division for his sixth victory. Finally, on the way to the rendezvous point following the strafing attacks, Louis Menard found and chased a 'Betty' bomber. He eventually shot it down into the sea, but not before he had suffered a minor leg wound from return fire.

Lt Cdr Torrey led 11 Hellcats off as escort to the first strike formation, but soon after leaving *Essex* the third division, comprising Lt 'Chick' Smith, Ens Lewis Matthews and Lt(jg) George Smith, was ordered to remain in the area as an emergency CAP. The division was given a vector about 15 miles away from the carrier, 'Chick' Smith leading the three fighters in the direction of approaching enemy aeroplanes. They soon intercepted two 'Betty' bombers, 'Chick' Smith opening fire on the lead aeroplane and sending it down in flames. George Smith and Lewis Matthews quickly dispatched the second 'Betty'. They then returned to *Essex* to continue their CAP.

Thirty minutes later the third division received another vector and dove down to intercept, passing over several ships in the carrier screen that had recently come under Japanese air attack. The ships opened fire, hitting Matthews' Hellcat as he flew behind the two Smiths. His fighter made a hard landing on the water, skipping several times, before plunging beneath the waves at a steep angle. Despite a search of the area Matthews was not found, and it was presumed that the young pilot had been killed in the crash.

The last strike of the day took off at 1330 hrs, with two divisions of Hellcats escorting eight torpedo-bombers and eight dive-bombers, while two more divisions escorted photographic aeroplanes. After recovering aircraft from this mission, TF 58 headed back to Majuro, where CAG-9 received the welcome news that it was to head back to the USA, having completed its combat cruise. En route to Pearl Harbor, the Carrier Air Group celebrated its second anniversary. VF-9 had established a commendable record during its second combat cruise, its pilots having claimed 120 Japanese aircraft shot down, with eight probably destroyed and an additional 124 destroyed on the ground. Ten pilots had become aces during the cruise, with Hamilton McWhorter returning as high scorer with ten victories, followed by Mayo Hadden with eight and Eugene Valencia with 7.5 claims. One pilot had been killed in action and four posted missing in action. Two more had been killed in flying accidents.

VF-9's second combat cruise had coincided with the formative months of the development of the US Navy's Fast Carrier Task Force, the promise from the first experimental probing attacks on Marcus and Wake becoming the reality of the well-executed, multi-carrier task group strikes on Truk and the Marianas. The naval historian G Clark Reynolds wrote that the raids on Truk and the Marianas 'revolutionised naval air warfare'.

These attacks demonstrated the mobility and power of American carrier forces that could now range across the Pacific to deliver punishing blows against Japanese bases and air power in support of amphibious operations. During the course of the squadron's seven months in the Pacific, VF-9 had helped establish beyond question the Hellcat's superiority over the Zero-sen, contributing to the 22-to-1 victory ratio enjoyed by US Navy carrier aircraft over their Japanese opponents in the first four months of 1944.

On the way back to Pearl Harbor VF-9 took several publicity shots of pilots sitting in a Hellcat with their victories marked below the cockpit. George Blair claimed three kills during the second combat cruise. He returned to action during the last few months of the war with VF-85, but his only claim was for a damaged 'Frank' on 2 June 1945 (*80G-217594, NARA*)

Lt(jg) Hamilton McWhorter, shown sitting in the same aircraft as George Blair, ended the cruise as both VF-9's leading scorer and the first double Hellcat ace with ten victory claims. He went on to score two more kills flying with VF-12 in 1945 (*80G-217597, NARA*)

THIRD COMBAT CRUISE

CAG-9 flew its aircraft off *Essex* just prior to the carrier reaching San Francisco on 10 March 1944. After physical exams and filling out paperwork, the men of the Carrier Air Group were given a welcome month's leave to be reunited with their families. In mid-April 1944, the veterans of VF-9 began arriving at NAS Pasco, in southeastern Washington State, to begin re-forming the squadron and CAG-9. Lt Cdrs Phil Torrey and Herbert Houck resumed their positions as CO of CAG-9 and CO of VF-9, respectively, but a number of pilots from the latter unit had moved on to other assignments. Matthew Byrnes, Reuben Denoff, John Franks, Hamilton McWhorter, Louis Menard and 'Chick' Smith had all been posted to VF-12, where they added to their scores in the aerial battles over Japan and Okinawa in 1945. Bill Bonneau, Marvin Franger and Eugene Valencia were promoted to the rank of lieutenant and made division leaders.

The veterans were charged with preparing a new crop of ensigns for combat, the neophyte fighter pilots having just graduated from operational training schools. Naval Aviators like Bonneau, Franger and Valencia not only passed on their experiences of combat to the ensigns, but also made sure that they had a healthy respect for their opponents – even with VF-9's undisputed success in aerial combat. Indeed, when interviewed for a local paper, Bill Bonneau stressed the importance of not underestimating a Japanese pilot, especially one flying a Zero-sen;

'The boys in our squadron learned long ago that the Zero, although vulnerable, must be treated with respect, and there's no sense in figuring that the Japanese flying it is any dumbbell. I've had plenty of scraps with

Lt Cdr Phil Torrey and his squadron commanders respond to questions from journalists after their return to Pearl Harbor in March 1944 (*80G-216622, NARA*)

the Japanese, and while some of them seem to be a bit lacking when it comes to grey matter, a lot of them are hitting on all eight cylinders all the time.'

Eugene Valencia echoed his friend's comments;

'When people here say the Japanese fighters are inferior, we get mad. People can say what they want, but we know the Jap Zero is still the best and the fastest aeroplane in the air. Those Japs know they are flying tinder boxes, and they've learned how to handle them. They don't take unnecessary

chances like they did at first, and they're darn good pilots.'

There was a great deal of training to be done. Many of the newer ensigns had never flown an F6F before, having been rushed through operational training following a fighter syllabus that culminated in time in the SBD Dauntless due to a shortage of Hellcats. The first order of business was to ensure that these new pilots became thoroughly familiar with the F6F. As an experiment, VB-9 had converted to the Hellcat too, so VF-9 had to share the available F6Fs with its sister-squadron, creating a constant scheduling challenge.

When all the newer pilots had completed conversion to the Hellcat, an intensive tactical training programme got underway covering gunnery, ground strafing, bombing, rocket firing and practice interceptions under the control of a fighter director. Air combat training concentrated on perfecting the 'Thach Weave' until it was second nature. As training progressed, VF-9 moved on to working with VB-9 and VT-9 on practice strikes. All the pilots went down to North Island near San Diego for carrier landing qualifications.

At the end of August VF-9 was informed that the complement for US Navy carrier fighter squadrons had been increased to 54 aeroplanes and 81 pilots. At the same time it was announced that VB-9 was to be re-formed with SB2C Helldivers. VF-9 acquired 31 new Naval Aviators through transfers from VB-9, quickly putting these former bomber pilots through a training programme in gunnery and air combat tactics.

As a division leader, Lt Eugene Valencia had the opportunity to try out the tactical ideas he had begun to form after his experience at Truk. Valencia selected three fresh young ensigns to form his division – James French, Joe Roquemore and Clinton Smith. Valencia devised a tactic he called the 'Mowing Machine' in which the two sections of a division or the two aeroplanes in a section

CAG-9 re-formed at NAS Pasco, Washington, and began an intensive training programme in preparation for its next combat cruise. VF-9 shared its F6F-3 Hellcats with VB-9, temporarily assigned to fly the big Grumman fighter. During August 1944 the squadron began to receive new F6F-5 Hellcats (*Pasco Historical Society*)

While at Pasco many VF-9 pilots received medals for their actions during the second combat cruise. Here, Lt Cdr Phil Torrey presents awards to the recently promoted Lts Eugene Valencia and Marvin Franger and Lt Cdr Herbert Houck (*80G-284755, NARA*)

alternated roles, the first section or aeroplane attacking an enemy aircraft formation while the second section or aeroplane remained above as top cover. As the first section pulled up and away from its attack, the second section would go down to attack while the first section provided cover, repeating the process again and again like the blades of a lawn mower going round and around. The result was to increase the offensive potential of the division, while at the same time providing maximum protection for the attacking section.

Valencia drilled his division relentlessly in his new tactic. He had his two sections split into 'friendly' and 'enemy' aeroplanes, and practised gunnery approaches from different angles while still using the 'Mowing Machine' tactic, perfecting their teamwork. Clinton Smith recalled later that when flying with Eugene Valencia, 'there never was a dull minute in the sky. All the way through training, if we were going to or from a mission, on the way we pulled tactics'.

Towards the end of September CAG-9 was alerted that it would soon be leaving the USA for the Pacific. The Carrier Air Group travelled to Pearl Harbor aboard *Yorktown*, arriving at Ford Island on 18 October 1944. For the next two months VF-9 and the rest of CAG-9 undertook intensive training, the fighters concentrating on gunnery, rocketing, bombing and tactics. There were several exercises involving the entire Carrier Air Group, which saw coordinated strikes being practised.

Tragically, prior to arriving in Hawaii, Ens Joe Roquemore had succumbed to pneumonia. Lt Valencia selected Ens Harris Mitchell, one of the VB-9 Hellcat pilots who had transferred over to VF-9, as his replacement. The weeks in Hawaii gave Valencia an opportunity to drill Mitchell in his 'Mowing Machine' tactics and integrate him into the division.

The training regime ended on 18 December so that CAG-9 could prepare to ship out to the Pacific. This prompted a squadron beer party, which included the liberal use of smoke bombs and a fire hose in the Base Officers' Quarters! On 20 December 1944, VF-9 and the rest of CAG-9 boarded the escort carrier USS *Munda* (CVE-104), which took them to Manus Island in the Admiralties. On the day VF-9 left Pearl Harbor, six specially trained pilots joined the unit to form a dedicated nightfighter flight. *Munda* arrived at Manus on 1 January 1945. CAG-9 moved to an airfield on Ponam Island off the north coast of Manus, where the squadrons began one last round of intensive training, concentrating on group air attacks.

As a result of the kamikaze attacks in the Philippines, at the end of 1944 the complement of the fleet carrier fighter squadrons was increased from 54 to 72 fighters, but this proved to be administratively unwieldy. These larger squadrons were then split into separate fighter and fighter-bomber squadrons. Shortly after arrival at Ponam Island, half of VF-9's pilots went to form a new fighter-bomber squadron – designated VBF-9 – that had a dual attack and fighter mission. VBF-9 was

VF-9 began its third combat cruise aboard USS *Lexington* (CV-16), spending the first few days aboard ship ironing out 'some kinks in our landings'. This F6F-5 was written off after the arrestor wire snapped on landing and it ran into the barrier erected to prevent aircraft from colliding with aeroplanes parked tightly on the bow of the ship (*National Naval Aviation Museum*)

commissioned on 8 January 1945, with Lt Cdr Frank Lawlor, a former American Volunteer Group ace, as commander. VF-9 and VBF-9 were each allocated 36 Hellcats, but in practice the two squadrons used aircraft interchangeably.

VF-9's first experience of island living was not what its pilots had expected. 'We soon found that Pacific island living was not romantic', the unit's War Diary recorded, 'but that the food was canned, water was salty and when the rain wasn't falling the sun was out to set a record'. CAG-9 left Manus, none too soon in the opinion of many, on 29 January 1945, travelling aboard the escort carrier USS *Barnes* (CVE-20) to the newest fleet anchorage at Ulithi Atoll. Arriving on 3 February, CAG-9 embarked in *Lexington*, replacing CAG-20 and taking over its F6F-5 Hellcats.

TOKYO

During its second combat cruise, VF-9 had played a part in the formation and validation of the Fast Carrier Task Force concept. Now the squadron would participate in the application of unprecedented naval power. Having smashed the IJN at the two battles of the Philippine Sea, the Fast Carrier Task Force was at the peak of its power, being the mightiest fleet the world had ever seen. Now back under its old designation as the Fifth Fleet's TF 58, with Adm Spruance and now Vice Adm Mitscher having taken over from Adm Halsey and Vice Adm John McCain, the Fast Carrier Task Force comprised four Carrier Task Groups with nine *Essex*-class and five *Independence*-class carriers, and a special night Carrier Task Group with *Enterprise* and *Saratoga*. *Lexington* was part of TG 58.2, with USS *Hancock* (CV-19) and USS *San Jacinto* (CVL-30).

The next major operation was the invasion of Iwo Jima, planned for 19 February 1945. After boarding *Lexington*, CAG-9's squadrons received detailed briefings on their role in the landings. Leaving Ulithi on 10 February, TG 58.2 expected to head for Iwo Jima, but to its surprise and consternation, the Task Group was informed that it would be targeting Tokyo instead.

As the VF-9 War Diary recorded, 'once underway we were given a real shock to learn that our first strike was to be against Tokyo. The squadron had some pensive men at that time. It was almost unbelievable – a strike against Tokyo itself'. The idea for the strike came from Adm Spruance, commander of the Fifth Fleet. A carrier strike on Tokyo would be a blow to Japanese morale, and it would hopefully result in the destruction of many enemy aircraft, keeping them away from the landings on Iwo Jima.

The deck crew fold the wings of an F6F-5 on *Lexington*. The white strip on the tail identified aircraft flying from CV-16 (*80G-319638, NARA*)

As he had done with previous strikes against Japanese bases, Mitscher planned to begin the day with fighter sweeps over the Tokyo area. VF-9 and the two other fighter squadrons in TG 58.2 were assigned to sweep the airfields northeast of Tokyo on the Chiba Peninsula. The pilots spent a lot of time going over their targets and their plan of attack.

At 0645 hrs on 16 February, when TG 58.2 was 115 miles southeast of Tokyo, *(text continues on page 63)*

1
F2A-3 Buffalo (BuNo unknown)/
black 9-F-6 of VF-9, East Field,
NAS Norfolk, Virginia, March
1942

2
F4F-4 Wildcat (BuNo unknown)/
black 9-F-2 of VF-9, USS *Ranger*
(CV-4), August–September 1942

3
F4F-4 Wildcat BuNo 11762/black
9-F-15 flown by Ens Louis
Menard, VF-9, USS *Ranger*
(CV 4), November 1942

53

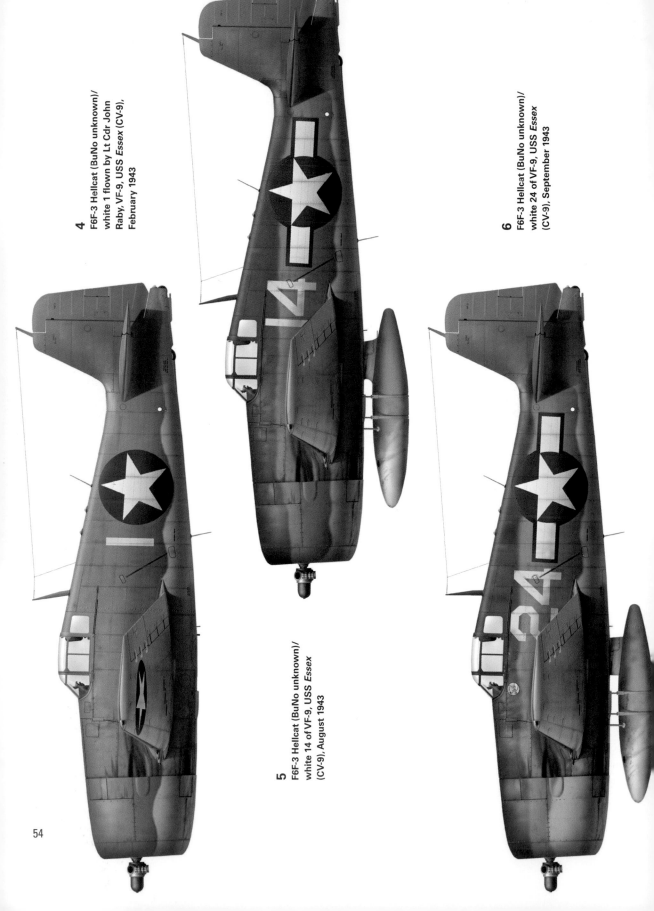

4
F6F-3 Hellcat (BuNo unknown) / white 1 flown by Lt Cdr John Raby, VF-9, USS *Essex* (CV-9), February 1943

5
F6F-3 Hellcat (BuNo unknown) / white 14 of VF-9, USS *Essex* (CV-9), August 1943

6
F6F-3 Hellcat (BuNo unknown) / white 24 of VF-9, USS *Essex* (CV-9), September 1943

7
F6F-3 Hellcat (BuNo unknown)/
white 17 of VF-9, USS *Essex*
(CV-9), October 1943

8
F6F-3 Hellcat BuNo 25900/white 7
flown by Lt(jg) Hamilton
McWhorter, VF-9, USS *Essex*
(CV-9), October 1943

9
F6F-3 Hellcat BuNo 40509/white 15
flown by Lt(jg) Hamilton
McWhorter, VF-9, USS *Essex*
(CV-9), January 1944

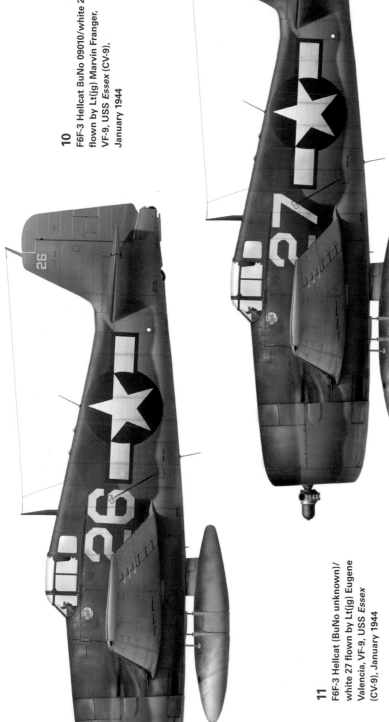

10
F6F-3 Hellcat BuNo 09010/white 26 flown by Lt(jg) Marvin Franger, VF-9, USS *Essex* (CV-9), January 1944

11
F6F-3 Hellcat (BuNo unknown)/white 27 flown by Lt(jg) Eugene Valencia, VF-9, USS *Essex* (CV-9), January 1944

12
F6F-3 Hellcat (BuNo unknown)/white 35 flown by Lt Leslie DeCew, VF-9, USS *Essex* (CV-9), January 1944

13
F6F-3 Hellcat (BuNo unknown)/
white 36 flown by Lt(jg) William
Bonneau, VF-9, USS *Essex*
(CV-9), February 1944

14
F6F-3 Hellcat BuNo 66056/white 22
flown by Lt(jg) Marvin Franger,
VF-9, USS *Essex* (CV-9),
February 1944

15
F6F-3 Hellcat (BuNo unknown)/
white 17 flown by Ens John
Franks, VF-9, USS *Essex* (CV-9),
February 1944

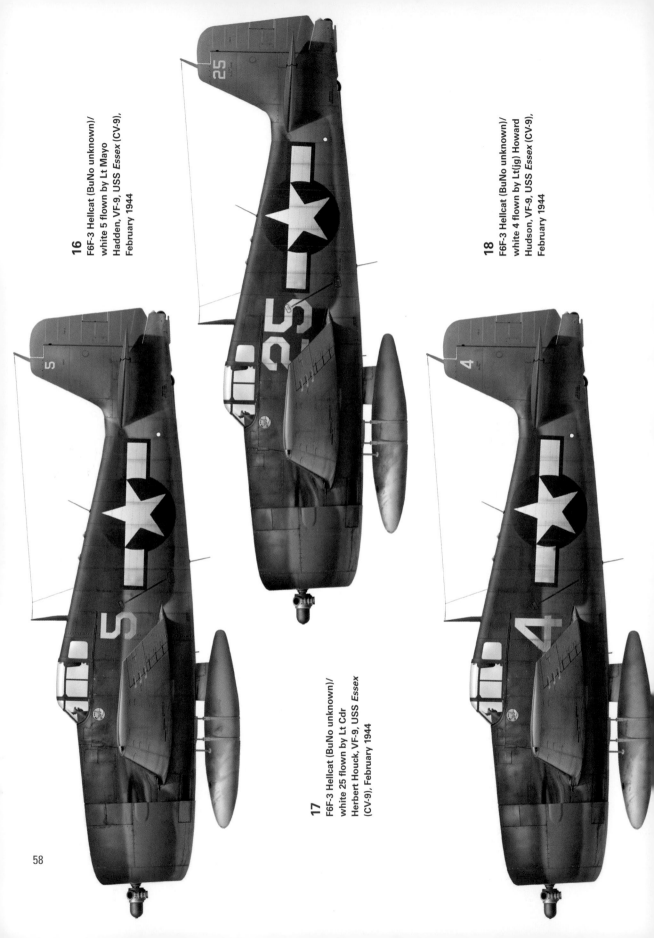

16
F6F-3 Hellcat (BuNo unknown)/
white 5 flown by Lt Mayo
Hadden, VF-9, USS *Essex* (CV-9),
February 1944

17
F6F-3 Hellcat (BuNo unknown)/
white 25 flown by Lt Cdr
Herbert Houck, VF-9, USS *Essex*
(CV-9), February 1944

18
F6F-3 Hellcat (BuNo unknown)/
white 4 flown by Lt(jg) Howard
Hudson, VF-9, USS *Essex* (CV-9),
February 1944

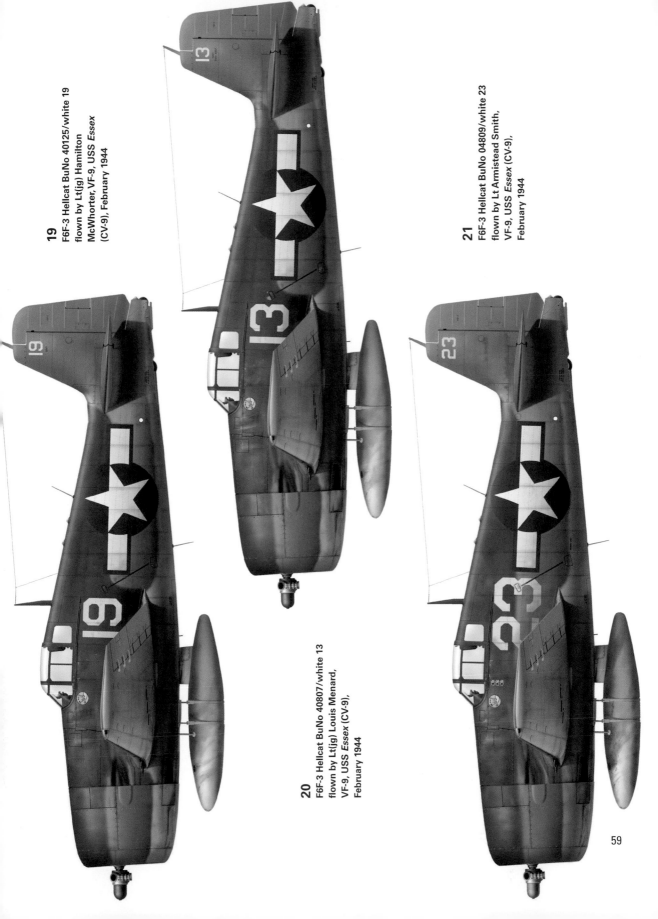

19
F6F-3 Hellcat BuNo 40125/white 19 flown by Lt(jg) Hamilton McWhorter, VF-9, USS *Essex* (CV-9), February 1944

20
F6F-3 Hellcat BuNo 40807/white 13 flown by Lt(jg) Louis Menard, VF-9, USS *Essex* (CV-9), February 1944

21
F6F-3 Hellcat BuNo 04809/white 23 flown by Lt Armistead Smith, VF-9, USS *Essex* (CV-9), February 1944

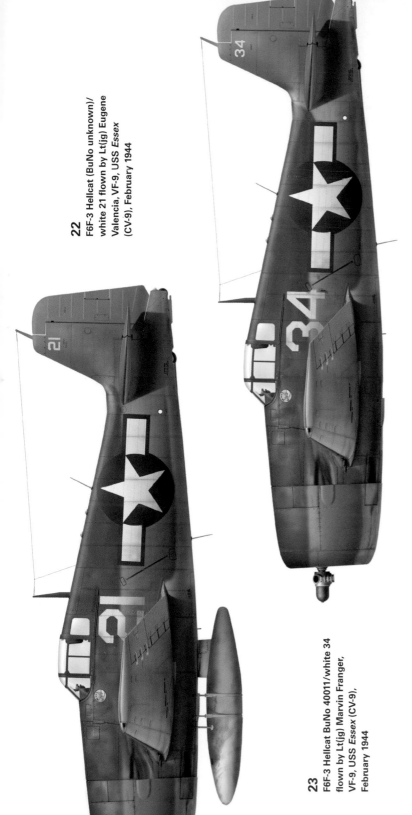

22
F6F-3 Hellcat (BuNo unknown)/
white 21 flown by Lt(jg) Eugene
Valencia, VF-9, USS *Essex*
(CV-9), February 1944

23
F6F-3 Hellcat BuNo 40011/white 34
flown by Lt(jg) Marvin Franger,
VF-9, USS *Essex* (CV-9),
February 1944

24
F6F-3 Hellcat (BuNo unknown)/
white 6 flown by Lt(jg)
Armistead Smith, VF-9, USS
Essex (CV-9), February 1944

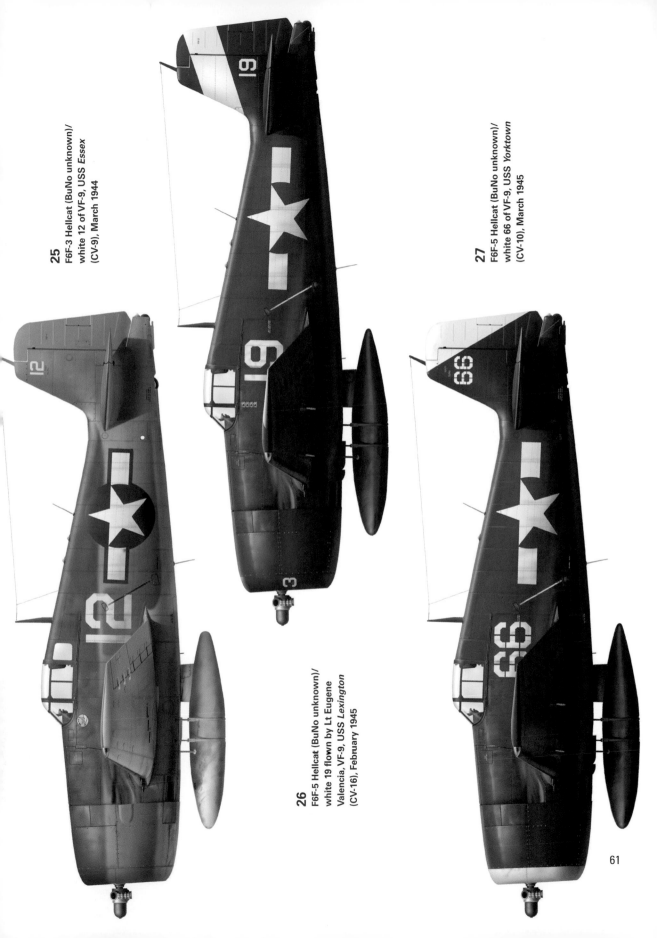

25
F6F-3 Hellcat (BuNo unknown)/
white 12 of VF-9, USS *Essex*
(CV-9), March 1944

26
F6F-5 Hellcat (BuNo unknown)/
white 19 flown by Lt Eugene
Valencia, VF-9, USS *Lexington*
(CV-16), February 1945

27
F6F-5 Hellcat (BuNo unknown)/
white 66 of VF-9, USS *Yorktown*
(CV-10), March 1945

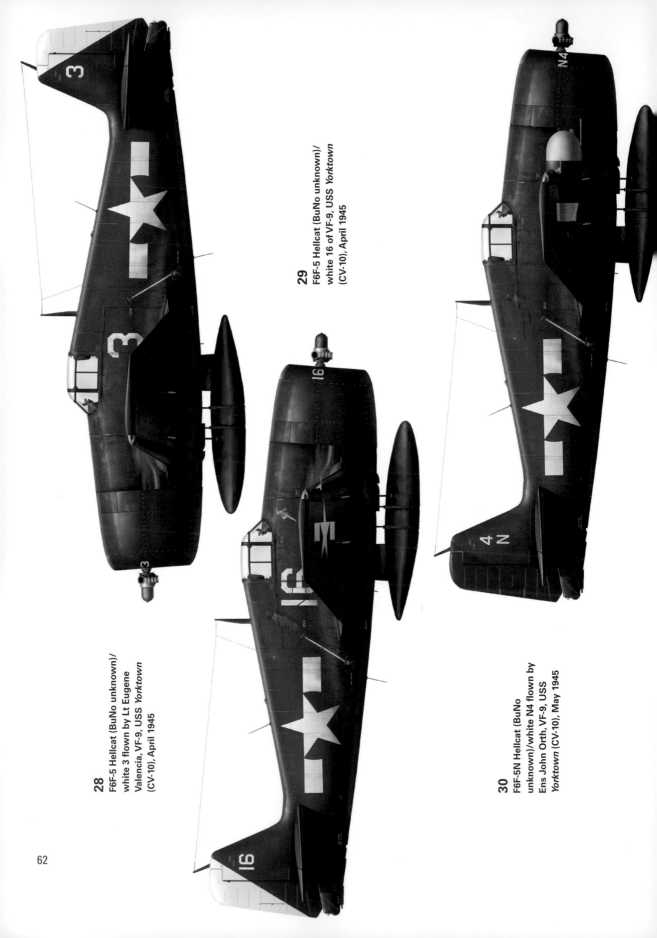

28
F6F-5 Hellcat (BuNo unknown)/
white 3 flown by Lt Eugene
Valencia, VF-9, USS *Yorktown*
(CV-10), April 1945

29
F6F-5 Hellcat (BuNo unknown)/
white 16 of VF-9, USS *Yorktown*
(CV-10), April 1945

30
F6F-5N Hellcat (BuNo
unknown)/white N4 flown by
Ens John Orth, VF-9, USS
Yorktown (CV-10), May 1945

Lt Cdr Houck took off with five divisions of F6F-5 Hellcats as part of Flight 2A. Lts Leslie DeCew, Howard Hudson, Marvin Franger and Philip Ball led the other divisions. The weather was poor – cold, with rain squalls and a ceiling down as low as 800 ft. Houck rendezvoused with 12 Hellcats from VF-80 off *Hancock* and eight from VF-45 off *San Jacinto* and headed west. As the formation crossed the coast and headed inland, the ceiling rose to 8000 ft, but Houck could see that their primary target – the airfield at Kisarazu on Tokyo Bay, on the west side of the Chiba Peninsula, was still weathered in. He led the formation northeast towards the airfield at Katori (some ten miles northeast of today's Narita airport) instead.

Keeping some aeroplanes above as cover, Houck led the others down to strafe the airfield, and in repeated passes claimed eight aircraft destroyed, six probably destroyed and an additional 12 damaged. Climbing back up to 7500 ft, Houck then flew southwest to strike at Mobara airfield, on the eastern side of the Chiba Peninsula. En route, the Hellcats ran into Japanese fighters.

Alerted to the approaching carrier fighters, the JAAF and the IJN reacted strongly. The former sent up several fighter sentai, among them the 47th with Nakajima Ki-84 Hayate ('Frank') fighters and the 23rd with Ki-43 'Oscars', while a large number of Zero-sens and new Kawanishi N1K2 Shiden-Kai ('George') from the 201st, 252nd, 302nd, 601st, Yokosuka and Tsukuba Kokutai intercepted Hellcat formations around Tokyo.

In its first contact, VF-9 ran into five or six fighters that pilots identified as Nakajima Ki 27 Type 97s ('Nates'). As the obsolete JAAF machines jumped the Hellcat formation, 20 to 25 'Zekes' also arrived on the scene. Despite a huge dogfight erupting, DeCew and Ball still managed to take their divisions down to strafe Mobara field – Marvin Franger and his division gave them cover. Both divisions claimed two aeroplanes destroyed on the ground, one probable and two damaged.

Above the strafers, the Hellcat pilots providing cover fought against repeated attacks from single Japanese aeroplanes coming in at them out of the clouds above and also from below. The Naval Aviators had to constantly weave in division- and section-strength in order to evade their attackers. Despite trying hard to keep formation integrity, Franger's

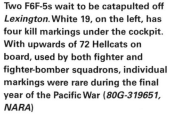

Two F6F-5s wait to be catapulted off *Lexington*. White 19, on the left, has four kill markings under the cockpit. With upwards of 72 Hellcats on board, used by both fighter and fighter-bomber squadrons, individual markings were rare during the final year of the Pacific War (*80G-319651, NARA*)

division gradually broke away to re-form at the rendezvous point, five miles off the east coast of the Chiba Peninsula. Once here, they ran into yet another melee. An indication of the intensity of the combat experienced during this mission is the fact that VF-9 submitted claims for 14 Japanese aeroplanes destroyed and no fewer than 23 damaged. The need to maintain a constant weave meant that many pilots could get off little more than a snap shot at an on-coming fighter – to dive down after a target in the middle of a melee was dangerous.

As Herbert Houck led his division to the rendezvous point after strafing Katori airfield, 'Zekes' started dropping out of the clouds. Houck got in a long burst at one of them as it approached him at the same altitude, firing a 45-degree deflection shot, but he soon found that only one of his machine guns was working – the cold weather over Japan caused a number of machine guns to freeze up. Houck watched the 'Zeke' fly past him smoking and then enter a dive, but with other enemy fighters around he could not go after it. Despite having only one gun working, he fired at several more 'Zekes' until his engine started cutting out, causing him to break off and return to the rendezvous point.

Houck's wingman, Ens Steve Cushing, became separated from his leader when his engine briefly cut out after it was hit in the carburettor. Cushing subsequently shot down one of the 'Nate' fighters, watching it explode in a head-on attack. He then joined up with Lt DeCew's division to strafe Mobara airfield.

Houck's other section also split up in the melee. Lt(jg) William Emerson was leading Ens Robert Parker when the 'Nate' fighters attacked. Emerson fired at one of them head on, seeing hits, but the 'Nate' dived away. When the 'Zekes' appeared, Emerson and Parker began a defensive weave. The former shot down one of them in a head-on attack, turning into the 'Zeke' as it came in on him at the same altitude. Emerson quickly resumed weaving with Parker, trying to join up with other Hellcats. When another 'Zeke' started a run on Parker from above Emerson pulled up and into it. The IJN pilot responded by pushing over into a dive, and in his exuberance Parker immediately rolled over and followed the Zeke down, firing as he got onto its tail. This was the last time Emerson saw him, Parker failing to return to *Lexington*. He had almost certainly fallen victim to yet another Japanese fighter.

Lt Leslie DeCew and his division also ran into the 'Nates' after pulling up from strafing Katori airfield. DeCew rolled in on one of them after a 'Nate' had attacked a Hellcat. Coming at him almost directly head on, DeCew fired and saw hits, shortly after which the JAAF pilot bailed out. This was DeCew's fifth victory of the war. His wingman, Lt(jg) Eston Baden, also claimed a 'Nate'. Continuing to go after the JAAF fighters, DeCew and Baden together damaged several more, while his second section shot down three 'Zekes' during the running battles. Lt Marvin Franger was also involved in the clash with the 'Nates', firing at one that he spotted coming directly at him. Getting hits in the engine and setting the 'Nate' on fire, he saw the fighter fly past him in flames. Moments later Franger's wingman confirmed that the 'Nate' had exploded. Marvin Franger's tally now stood at six kills.

Lt Howard Hudson's division fought a hard but frustrating battle. Hudson had two victories from VF-9's second combat cruise, and narrowly missed becoming an ace this day. In the first part of the melee with the Japanese fighters, Hudson made two stern attacks and two head-on attacks against the 'Nates', hitting four of them, but he failed to knock any down. A short time later he latched onto the tail of a 'Zeke' and hit i.s right wing before the fighter broke away. Hudson and his wingman, Ens William McLaurin, then spotted a Nakajima Ki-46 Type 100 reconnaissance aeroplane ('Dinah'), which appears to have blundered into the melee and immediately headed for the clouds above. Hudson and McLaurin gave chase, McLaurin getting hits on the 'Dinah's' wings and engines, setting it on fire and sending it down to crash.

Lt(jg) Henry Champion, another veteran from VF-9's 1943-44 combat cruise, was leading the second section. He had not had an opportunity to score any victories during the earlier cruise, and the fighter sweep on 16 February proved to be the biggest combat he saw during the war. To Champion's immense frustration his fighter's guns were not working properly. 'I had a bad day that day', he remembered. 'I shot at quite a few aeroplanes, but checking our guns going in I could only get three to work. This meant that I didn't have quite the firepower needed to knock them down. I fired on at least 12 aeroplanes, and should have gotten all of them!'

With only three guns working, Champion damaged four 'Nates' and then got good hits on two 'Zekes' as they came at him head-on. Both IJN fighters flew past him trailing smoke, but they were soon out of sight. As another 'Zeke' came in on him, Champion opened fire, getting hits in the engine and the cockpit area. The 'Zeke' began to burn and seemed out of control, as if the pilot had been hit. Champion quickly turned and came around on its tail and, with two more bursts from his three working guns, the 'Zeke' exploded for Champion's first victory.

At 1045 hrs Cdr Phil Torrey, CO of CAG-9, led off the second fighter sweep from *Lexington*, 12 VF-9 Hellcats joining up with 12 from VF-80 and eight from VF-45 after takeoff. The weather remained poor over the Task Group, with cold rain and ten-tenths overcast at 800 ft. As the formation neared the Japanese coast, the ceiling lifted to around 8000 ft, but a light haze down to the ground limited visibility. The target for this second sweep was the airfield at Imba, in the same general area as the earlier fighter sweep. Torrey led the formation on a wide circle around the airfield and, seeing no enemy fighters and no anti-aircraft fire, he ordered the divisions to go down to strafe the target.

As Torrey entered a dive, other pilots called out Japanese fighters coming in. He began a defensive weave, and those Hellcats carrying rockets quickly jettisoned them in the direction of the airfield. For the next 40 minutes the Hellcat pilots came under continuous attack by small formations of 'Zekes' and Ki-61 'Tonys', the latter most likely from the 244th Sentai.

This mission marked the debut of Lt Eugene Valencia's division, and he and his new pilots did well in their first engagement of VF-9's third combat cruise. Indeed, Valencia's division was the first to be attacked, a lone Nakajima Ki-44 Type 2 fighter ('Tojo') targeting the division in a steep dive from astern. Valencia led his men in a 180-degree turn to counter the attack and, upon coming out of this defensive manoeuvre, Lt(jg) Harris Mitchell, flying as Valencia's wingman, was in a perfect position to engage the Ki-44. Opening fire, he saw hits on the JAAF fighter that caused the Japanese pilot to bail out, giving future ace Mitchell his first victory.

Immediately thereafter three 'Tonys' attacked Valencia's division, and the sections became separated from each other and from the rest of the VF-9 formation as they fought off their attackers. During this clash Valencia shot down one of the Ki-61s for his first victory of the third cruise. The 'Tony' came in on Valencia from astern but missed him during his attack, the JAAF pilot then flying directly across the nose of the Hellcat as he pulled out. Valencia fired a long burst after manoeuvring onto the 'Tony's' tail, getting hits in its cockpit and radiator. The Ki-61 began smoking, then burst into flames and went down.

Lt(jg) Jim French and his wingman Lt(jg) Clinton Smith (Valencia's second section) got split up as they battled the 'Tonys'. French shot down one of them, getting onto the tail of the Japanese fighter following a tight turn and setting it on fire with hits in the wings. At this point he became worried when he could not locate his wingman. French called Cdr Torrey to check to see if Smith was at the rendezvous point, but got no answer, so he headed out on his own, where he joined up with the others. French was relieved to find Smith at the rendezvous. 'I thought he'd had it', French recalled, 'but luckily we joined up again at the rendezvous point. He signalled to me that he had shot down his first Jap. I had, too, so we were both pretty happy'. Smith had shot down a 'Tony' that was making a pass on another division, turning into the Japanese fighter and sending it down in flames.

Lt Bill Bonneau shot down an 'Oscar' for his eighth, and last, kill of the war, seeing the pilot bail out. In the chaotic combat that followed, Bonneau also damaged three 'Zekes' and a 'Tony' as they pulled up from attacks on other Hellcat formations. His wingman, Lt(jg) Walter Andrews, damaged a 'Zeke', two 'Tonys' and a 'Tojo' while following his section leader. Lt William Hilkane, leading the second section in Bonneau's division, was seen to destroy a 'Zeke' during the combat. He then told his division leader over the radio that he was out of ammunition. Bonneau ordered him to head to the rendezvous point to the east, but Hilkane and his wingman became briefly separated from the rest of the formation and were bounced by six 'Zekes'. One of them hit Hilkane's Hellcat hard, causing an explosion in the cockpit. The fighter duly crashed into the sea,

Lt Eugene Valencia and his division. They are, from left to right, Lt(jg) Harris Mitchell, Lt Valencia, Lt(jg) James French and Lt(jg) Clinton Smith. Harris came from VB-9 to replace Ens Joe Roquemore, who succumbed to pneumonia before VF-9 reached Hawaii. The division saw its first action during the February 1945 strikes on Tokyo (*via the author*)

Hilkane going in with his Hellcat. His wingman escaped with a high-speed dive down to the sea.

There was one more loss from the mission. At 1225 hrs, as the Japanese fighter attacks began to diminish, Cdr Torrey led his division north towards Imba airfield. Torrey had not apparently hit any Japanese aircraft, although his wingman, Lt(jg) Donald Kent, had damaged three fighters and the leader of Torrey's second section, Lt Edward McGowan, who had 3.5 claims from aerial battles during the Rabaul mission, had destroyed one 'Tony' and damaged a second, with his wingman getting a 'Tojo'. As the division headed north, a single Ki-44 dove out of the clouds directly toward Torrey's aircraft in a head-on run. Torrey and the Japanese pilot opened fire as they raced towards each other, the 'Tojo' breaking off in a 'split-S' to the right.

A few minutes later Torrey's aeroplane began a series of steep dives and climbs. Kent tried to follow his leader, but at the top of the third climb he stalled and spun out. He last saw Torrey at the bottom of his third dive, just beginning to pull up. Kent turned to get in position to join up with his leader, but lost sight of him. Torrey failed to return from the mission. In all likelihood he had been severely wounded in the attack, or possibly in a previous encounter, as no damage to his Hellcat was evident. His loss was a blow to morale, for Cdr Philip Torrey had been a capable and well-respected leader. Writing to Torrey's wife, Lt Cdr Houck said how much he would be missed. 'He was a wonderful fellow', he wrote, 'as a friend, as a leader and as an example. Phil always flew more than his fair share of combat missions. In all of them he acquitted himself admirably'.

Despite the loss of its CO, CAG-9 continued to send out aircraft to strike targets around Tokyo. At 1400 hrs, Lt Jack Kitchen (VF-9's Executive Officer) led four divisions to escort Helldivers and Avengers sent to bomb the Nakajima aircraft factory at Ota, northwest of Tokyo. This was a large operation, with 13 SB2Cs from VB-9, 14 TBMs from VT-9 and a contingent of 12 F6Fs and nine TBMs from VF-45 and VT-45, respectively, being involved. Nine of the VF-9 Hellcats carried rockets. The formation reached the target without interference and bombed successfully, the Hellcats firing their rockets into the factory complex.

As the carrier aircraft headed for the rendezvous point off the coast, 25 Japanese fighters made attacking runs at the formation, targeting any aeroplane that lagged behind. The Hellcats went into a defensive weave over the dive- and torpedo-bombers and kept the Japanese fighters at bay. Lt Leslie DeCew reacted to a 'Zeke' that was making feint attacks on the formation he was escorting. When it came in closer, DeCew turned and got on the 'Zeke's' tail, hitting it in the engine area. The 'Zeke' went down smoking and crashed for DeCew's second kill of the day, and his sixth victory of the war. A little later DeCew damaged a 'Frank' that was making a stern attack on a straggling TBM, the JAAF fighter pulling up in a loop just as DeCew opened fire. He saw hits in the fuselage and the wings before the 'Frank' dived away.

The next day (17 February) Lt Cdr Houck took over as commander of CAG-9 and Lt Jack Kitchen moved up to become CO of VF-9. Houck led his first mission as Carrier Air Group commander that morning, taking 14 Hellcats from VF-9 and 12 from VF-80 on a repeat fighter sweep east of Tokyo. Mechanical problems forced a number of pilots to turn back short of the target, leaving Houck with only two divisions – his own and Eugene Valencia's. Weather was again poor, and haze and low fog covered the

Japanese airfields, preventing a strike on Kisarazu. Houck led his two divisions to Mobara airfield instead, where the weather had cleared sufficiently to allow them to make a high strafing attack.

After the attack Houck climbed to 14,000-15,000 ft and was heading toward Katori airfield when both divisions ran into around 20 Japanese fighters. Houck ordered the divisions to begin weaving, which proved to be an effective defence, each section covering the other. Houck claimed one 'Zeke' with a full deflection shot in the running fight that followed. The fighter had passed from left to right in front of him, Houck opening fire and his bullets hitting the 'Zeke' in the engine and cockpit. The IJN pilot then attempted a 'split-S' manoeuvre to escape, but Houck pushed over and fired again, hitting the 'Zeke' in the port wing and setting it on fire. Moments later Houck's wingman saw the fighter explode. This turned out to be Houck's sixth, and last, claim of the war.

In the same fight Eugene Valencia scored twice. Seeing a 'Zeke' making an attack on Houck's second section, he chased after the Japanese fighter as it passed by the section and went into a diving spiral. Valencia began firing at deflection angle of 90 degrees, which he eventually pulled around to 30 degrees. Seeing smoke pouring from the 'Zeke's' cockpit, Valencia broke off his attack. Flying close behind him, Jim French saw the 'Zeke' pilot bail out. Five minutes later Valencia knocked down another fighter attacking Houck's section. An 'Oscar' had dived down on Houck from the 'one o'clock' position, and Valencia pulled up to meet the attack and got in a long burst of fire. Hitting the Ki-43 all over its fuselage and wings, the VF-9 ace watched the now flaming 'Oscar' spin down into the cloud base below.

This proved to be CAG-9's last mission to the Tokyo area. The next day the carriers steamed south to provide support for the landings on Iwo Jima.

Hellcats, Avengers and Helldivers of CAG-9 crowd the flightdeck of *Lexington* during the early spring of 1945. VF-9 and VBF-9 used Hellcats on board interchangeably (*80G-471808, NARA*)

CAG-9 began providing CAS for the landings on 19 February 1945 (the amphibious assault had commenced at 0900 hrs that morning), taking one day to refuel and re-arm (20th), before hitting Japanese positions again and again on 21 and 22 February – the unit expended hundreds of bombs and rockets, and made countless strafing attacks. The Marines on Iwo Jima had a high opinion of the Fast Carrier Task Force's ability to provide effective CAS.

On 23 February Adm Mitscher took TF 58 back up to Japan for more strikes against Tokyo, but bad weather caused the cancellation of all missions two days later. Four VF-9 divisions had, however, struggled through rain and low cloud to strafe the airfield at Konioke, damaging several hangars with bombs and rockets. Continuing poor weather forced the cancellation of planned strikes against Nagoya on 26 February too. On the way back to the fleet anchorage at Ulithi, TF 58 struck targets in the Ryukyu Islands. While aircraft from other Task Groups hit Okinawa, CAG-9 was assigned targets on nearby Amami Shima and Kikai Shima to the north of Okinawa.

TF 58 eventually returned to Ulithi on 4 March. Upon its arrival CAG-9 found that *Lexington* had been ordered to return to the USA for refit and repairs, the Carrier Air Group transferring to *Yorktown* – its old travelling companion – to replace CAG-3. The squadrons had a few days to settle in to operations from *Yorktown* before TF 58 headed out for its next operation, the invasion of Okinawa.

VF-9 transferred to USS *Yorktown* (CV-10) on 6 March 1945 to relieve CAG-3, spending several days conducting intensive flying operations to become familiar with the carrier's procedures (*80G-320164, NARA*)

⎯⎯⎯⎯⎯⎯⎯⎯ Okinawa ⎯⎯⎯⎯⎯⎯⎯⎯

Reflecting on the factors that make a fighter ace, Mike Hadden had no hesitation in stating that opportunity, being in 'the right place at the right time', was the most important element. Relative flying skill meant little

without enemy fighters to shoot at. Hadden had known pilots whom he considered to be better flyers and better shots than he was, but who had had the misfortune never to have encountered enemy aeroplanes. VF-9's experience during the Okinawa campaign reflects this truism.

For the first month of the campaign, from the preliminary strikes against Japanese airfields on Kyushu until the middle of April, the squadron's pilots had comparatively few opportunities to engage enemy aircraft. During this period VF-9 claimed only 22 Japanese aircraft destroyed. By one of those quirks of fate, VF-9 missed the three most intense days of air combat over Okinawa – 6, 12 and 16 April 1945 – which ranked among the US Navy's top ten highest daily claims of the war. But in the weeks that followed, the squadron more than made up for this relative drought, adding 78.5 claims to end the campaign as the second-highest scoring Hellcat squadron in TF 58. The majority of these claims – 68.5 – came during just three missions over a period of 24 days.

The invasion of Okinawa, codenamed Operation *Iceberg*, was the largest amphibious assault of the Pacific War. To seize the island, the US Navy amassed a fleet of some 1400 ships of all categories, with a landing force comprising three US Marine Corps and three US Army divisions. TF 58 employed 11 *Essex*-class fleet carriers and six *Independence*-class light carriers in its four Task Groups, with some 850 Hellcat and Corsairs being embarked in these vessels. The British Pacific Fleet's TF 57 provided additional support.

The Japanese high command greatly feared the loss of Okinawa, as its capture by the Allies would provide American forces with a base from which to launch the invasion of the home islands. The plan for the defence of Okinawa incorporated the use of mass kamikaze attacks combined with conventional attacks on Allied ships supporting the landing. The mass kamikaze strikes were designated Kikusui (Floating Chrysanthemum). The kamikaze threat, first seen during the campaign in the Philippines in

On 18 March 1945 VF-9 participated in the major strikes against Japanese airfields on Kyushu. Lt Cdr Houck led CAG-9 to attack the airfield at Oita, the Carrier Air Group claiming 17 aircraft destroyed on the ground (*Record Group 38, Box 347, Carrier Air Group Nine, NARA*)

VF-9 and VF-10 strafed the airfield at Usa on 18 March 1945. The VF-9 pilots claimed three aeroplanes destroyed and 15 damaged during the attack (*Record Group 38, Box 347, Carrier Air Group Nine, NARA*)

October 1944, put a heavy burden on the fleet carriers, who would have to combine offensive strikes with defensive CAPs over the fleet. The increase in fighter squadron complement to 72 aircraft at the end of 1944 was a direct result of this need for even more aeroplanes (for a more detailed discussion of the kamikaze and the air battles over Okinawa see *Osprey Aircraft of the Aces 109 – American Aces Against the Kamikaze*).

In preparation for the invasion of Okinawa, scheduled for 1 April 1945, Adm Mitscher planned two days of strikes against Japanese airfields on Kyushu – the home island nearest to Okinawa, and prospective base for the expected kamikaze attacks – and against remnants of the IJN fleet at its main base at Kure.

TF 58 sortied from Ulithi on 14 March 1945, with *Yorktown* forming part of TG 58.4. Over the next several days pilots received intensive briefings on their targets on Kyushu and Okinawa. On the morning of 18 March TF 58 stood off Kyushu and began launching its first strikes at around 0700 hrs. CAG-9 was assigned three airfields on the northeastern section of Kyushu at Oita, Usa and Tsuiki. For the first mission of the day Lt Cdr Houck led four divisions from VF-9 as escort to 12 SB2Cs from VB-9 and 13 TBMs from VT-9 that were targeting Oita airfield. The weather over the target area was only fair, but Houck found a hole in the clouds and led the formation down to strafe the airfield, the pilots claiming one single-engined and two twin-engined aircraft destroyed and several more damaged.

At 1000 hrs Lt DeCew led three divisions from VF-9 and three divisions of F4U Corsairs from VF-10 off *Intrepid* to strafe the airfield at Usa. In two passes the VF-9 pilots destroyed three aircraft and damaged an additional 15. At the same time, Lt Jack Kitchen took three divisions to the airfield at Tsuiki. Crossing the coast en route to the target, pilots in the formation saw two 'Vals' and a fighter they identified as a 'Nate' (more likely to have been a Mitsubishi Navy Type 96 Fighter). Kitchen's wingman and second section leader claimed one of the 'Vals' and the fighter as probably destroyed. The pilot of the second 'Val' made a miraculous escape from the fire of five Hellcats, for despite Kitchen's and Lt McGowan's divisions all firing on it, getting hits in the wings, the 'Val' pilot dropped down to the ground and made his escape by flying around low hills. The divisions went on to strafe hangars and aeroplanes on the airfield, claiming two single-engined trainers destroyed and 19 aeroplanes damaged.

Upon returning to the carrier, Eugene Valencia found that his tailhook would not extend, and he then had to circle while the Task Group came under attack. Running out of fuel, he ditched successfully and was picked up by one of the destroyers in the screen.

71

Most of the aerial combat that day had taken place over southern Kyushu, TF 58 squadrons submitting claims for 124 Japanese aircraft destroyed.

On 19 March the attacks shifted to the naval base at Kure and its surrounding airfields. VF-9 participated in two airfield strikes. At 0545 hrs Lt DeCew led four VF-9 divisions, and three from VF-10, in a fighter sweep over Kure airfield and Saijo and Matsuyama airfields on nearby Shikoku Island. Over Kure airfield the formation ran into intense and accurate flak, but it still went down to strafe the airfield installations with bombs, rockets and machine guns, destroying and damaging several aircraft. Moving on to

A Hellcat returning to *Yorktown* from one of the airfield strikes on 18 March 1945 heads for the barrier after the arrestor wires failed to bring it to a stop. For identification purposes, TF 58 painted a white ring around the cowl of the Hellcats and Corsairs participating in the two days of strikes against the island of Kyushu (*80G-328318, NARA*)

After the airfield attacks on 18 March VF-9 joined in the attacks on the IJN base at Kure and airfields on Shikoku Island the next day (*Record Group 38, Box 347, Carrier Air Group Nine, NARA*)

CAG-9's scoreboard, affixed to the superstructure of *Yorktown* in late March 1945, included claims made by both VF-9 and VBF-9 – the latter unit was credited with 51 aerial victories, five of them scored by its sole ace, Lt Edgar B McClure (*80G-376149, NARA*)

As part of the pre-invasion strikes against Okinawa, VF-9 attacked targets on other islands in the Ryukyu chain leading down to Okinawa from Kyushu. On 30 March the squadron conducted a sweep over Amami Island. Here, a VF-9 Hellcat flies toward the island beneath a low overcast (*Record Group 38, Box 347, Carrier Air Group Nine, NARA*)

Saijo airfield, the VF-9 divisions attacked hangars and aircraft. Lt(jg) Richard Prior was killed during one of the passes when his Hellcat lost its fin, rudder and horizontal stabiliser as he pulled out of his dive at 200 ft over the airfield, the aircraft having possibly been hit by anti-aircraft fire. Prior's Hellcat tumbled down and crashed into a hangar.

After this attack DeCew led his formation to strafe Matsuyama airfield. En route, Lt Bert Eckard's division ran into a small group of six to ten Japanese fighters, and a running fight ensued. Eckard destroyed a fighter he identified as a 'Frank', which, in all likelihood, was a Kawanishi N1K2 Shiden Kai ('George') from the 301st Sento Hikotai of the 343rd Kokutai, based at Matsuyama. This IJN squadron was heavily engaged against American carrier aircraft attacking Kure that morning, and it may be that the formation Eckard's division ran into was a group of 'George' fighters returning to their airfield. One of the enemy aircraft made a stern attack on Eckard, but misjudged his attack. As the 'George' flew past him, Eckard opened fire and the fighter started smoking. Ens Joseph Kaelin, Eckard's wingman, saw the N1K2 crash, giving future ace Eckard his first victory.

Kaelin made his first claim shortly thereafter when he opened fire on a fighter he identified as a 'Zeke' that had made a run on another Hellcat. Kaelin fired one long burst at the enemy fighter, then got in two more short bursts. The Japanese machine caught fire, started smoking and then erupted in flames once again, heading straight down. Kaelin then went after another fighter that

This Hellcat from VF-9 had its wing holed by flak while flying a mission over Okinawa in early April (*80G-376162, NARA*)

he identified as a 'Tojo' (again, most likely another 'George'), claiming this one as a probable. After the combat, in which his other section claimed two more 'Zekes' destroyed, Eckard and his division returned to the carrier. Meanwhile, after strafing Matsuyama airfield, DeCew led his three divisions back to Saijo airfield for a second strafing attack.

In total, VF-9 pilots claimed five aeroplanes destroyed, 12 probably destroyed and 45 damaged in the attacks. Coming off his strafing run on Saijo airfield, Lt Marvin Franger got in behind a 'Jake' floatplane that had inexplicably taken off in the middle of the attack. Getting in behind the aircraft as it was in a climbing turn, Franger opened fire with a 60 degree deflection shot and the 'Jake' crashed into the sea for the Hellcat ace's eighth victory.

VF-9 pilots rest in the squadron ready room between missions (*80G-333335, NARA*)

After additional strikes against Kyushu were postponed due to severe damage inflicted on USS *Franklin* (CV-13) by a solitary enemy bomber (807 sailors were killed and 487 wounded when fire and explosions ripped through the vessel's hangar deck), TF 58 headed back to Okinawa to begin pre-invasion strikes. En route, VF-9 pilots shot down three Japanese bombers on 21 March, including the first victory for VF-9's nightfighter flight – a 'Betty' bomber credited to Lt Dale Knopf during a night CAP.

Deck crews rest under the wings of two Hellcats spotted for the next CAP from *Yorktown* (*80G-333366, NARA*)

CAG-9 began strikes against Okinawa on 23 March 1945 when 22 Hellcats from VF-9 escorted 13 SB2Cs from VB-9 and 14 TBMs from VT-9 in an attack on the airfield at Naha. Poor weather, with ten-tenths cloud and heavy rain squalls, thwarted the attack, however. Despite less than ideal meteorological conditions, VF-9 flew repeated missions over Okinawa against airfields, anti-aircraft gun positions and other targets on the 24th and 25th, combining these sorties with strikes on the islands to the north. On 26 March the squadron escorted SB2Cs from VB-9 in a strike on Naha airport that also saw F4Us of VF-10 and SB2Cs from VB-10 attacking the same target. Lt(jg) Tom Connor's F6F was hit by anti-aircraft fire while making a strafing run on the airfield and he failed to return to the carrier. The airfield strikes continued after the successful landings on 1 April.

VF-9's nightfighters scored again on 5 April during a night intruder patrol over the airfield on Miyako Island, in the Sakishima Islands chain. TG 58.4 had taken over the duty of covering the Sakishima Islands for two days while TF 57 refuelled. Ens Jack Schwinn and future ace Ens John Orth were circling over the island when they saw the lighting system on the airfield come on. Splitting up, they orbited the field watching for enemy aircraft. Soon they saw two twin-engined aircraft approaching. Schwinn went in and shot down a 'Betty' bomber on its approach to the airfield. Orth, meanwhile, intercepted the second aeroplane, a Nakajima J1N1 Gekko ('Irving'), scoring hits that forced the IJN pilot to make a violent turn in an attempt to escape. Orth continued after the 'Irving', firing again and seeing more hits on the wing and fuselage. The aeroplane rolled over and crashed. A short while later Schwinn shot down a second 'Irving'.

During the day VF-9 carried out three sweeps over the islands despite bad weather, Lt Jack Kitchen leading four divisions in strafing attacks on various airfields that resulted in a number of enemy aeroplanes being damaged on the ground. Anti-aircraft fire knocked down Ens Howard Hudspeth and Lt(jg) Eston Baden, and although both Naval Aviators made successful water landings, only Hudspeth was rescued.

TG 58.4 returned to the Okinawa area on 7 April, VF-9 having missed the first Kikusui mission of the day before that had seen US Navy and Marine Corps carrier fighter pilots claim 257 Japanese aircraft shot down. On the 7th Lt Cdr Houck led CAG-9 in the attack on the

Japanese battleship *Yamato* and its screen as they attempted to make their own kamikaze sortie in defence of Okinawa. While the fighters strafed and bombed the Japanese warships, VB-9 and VT-9 administered the *coup de grâce* to *Yamato* and the cruiser *Agano*.

That afternoon two divisions undertook the first of many target CAPs around Okinawa. Lt Eugene Valencia's division spotted a Yokosuka P1Y Ginga ('Frances') and gave chase as the medium bomber dove down to wave-top height. The Hellcat pilots were using water injection, but after five minutes they had still not caught up with the fast 'Frances'. Finally, in desperation, Valencia shot off a burst of machine-gun fire in the 'Frances''

Aeroplanes of CAG-9 go after the Japanese cruiser *Agano* on 7 April 1945 during the attack on the battleship *Yamato*. Under Lt Cdr Herbert Houck's direction, CAG-9 helped administer the *coup de grâce* to the superbattleship and its escorts (*Record Group 38, Box 347, Carrier Air Group Nine, NARA*)

In January 1945 VF-9 was split into two separate fighter and fighter-bomber squadrons. VF-9's complement of aircraft was revised to incorporate a nightfighter flight of four F6F-5N Hellcats and six nightfighter pilots. VF-9 identified its nightfighters by adding an N to the aircraft tactical number. Here, one of the squadron's F6F-5Ns loses a tyre on landing (*80G-312546, NARA*)

LEFT A cockpit view of Hellcats about to launch on a mission. On its third combat cruise VF-9 appears not to have painted the squadron insignia on its F6F-5 Hellcats (*National Naval Aviation Museum*)

general direction, causing it to enter a shallow turn to the left. Jim French, leading the second section, crossed over Valencia and started firing at the 'Frances', getting some hits and forcing it to lose speed. Harris Mitchell (Valencia's wingman) then came in and finished the bomber off, sending it down to crash into the sea.

Another CAP on 11 April brought Lt(jg) Clinton Smith his second victory when he shot down a 'Zeke' while flying with Jim French. Finding the solitary IJN fighter below a layer of cloud, French had fired first and then had to swerve to avoid overshooting the aircraft. Smith came in right behind him and set the 'Zeke' on fire. The next day VF-9 shot down three Japanese fighters during a CAP over the airfield on Tokuna Island, in the Amami Island group, but again missed the big fight during the second Kikusui mission when US Navy and Marine Corps pilots claimed 144 Japanese aircraft destroyed.

On 16 April, the date of the third Kikusui mission, VF-9 was north of Okinawa on a fighter sweep against the airfields at Kagoshima and Izumi on southern Kyushu, so it again missed the third great aerial battle of the campaign. Pulling out of his strafing run over Kagoshima airfield, Eugene Valencia saw a 'Judy' dive-bomber fly out of a cloud layer ahead of him. He dove after the aeroplane, whose pilot made a left and right turn and then, as Valencia got into firing range, attempted a 'split-S' to escape, but failed to recover and crashed. VF-9's Air Intelligence Officer apparently refused to award Valencia a victory on the grounds that he had not fired on the Japanese machine.

On a dusk patrol that evening, Lt Dale Knopf of the nightfighter flight shot down a 'Frances' and another unidentified twin-engined aeroplane, and damaged a third.

77

VALENCIA'S 'FLYING CIRCUS'

VF-9's comparative lack of opportunity during its operations off Okinawa ended on 17 April 1945. That morning, at 0625 hrs, *Yorktown* sent out three divisions on CAP. Lts Eugene Valencia and Glenn Phillips were ordered to take their divisions to a point 50 miles north of TG 58.4, with Phillips patrolling at 10,000 ft and Valencia higher up at 20,000 ft. After an hour of circling, *Yorktown*'s radar picked up a large 'bogey' heading south toward the Task Group. Alerted, Valencia led his division in the direction of the approaching enemy formation.

At 0700 hrs the IJN's 5th Koku Kantai (Air Fleet) had ordered off a force of 62 Zero-sen fighters, 13 Suisei ('Judy') dive-bombers, 30 kamikaze aircraft, four Ginga ('Frances') medium bombers and 34 Shiden Kai ('George') fighters to attack units of TF 58 located northeast of Okinawa. The Shiden Kai fighters were to clear the way for the kamikaze aeroplanes. It seems probable that this was the formation that Valencia's division intercepted.

Lt(jg) Clinton Smith was apparently the first to see the oncoming Japanese formation, calling out 'bogeys' at 'three o'clock' to the rest of his division, which was flying below him at around 15,000 ft. Jim French and Clinton Smith were in a better position than Valencia and his wingman, Harris Mitchell, so, as they had practised countless times before, French turned towards the Japanese aircraft and led the attack. As they got closer, Valencia could see that the formation consisted of around 40 fighters, which he identified as 'Franks' and 'Zekes', but which may well have been a mixed formation of 'Georges' and 'Zekes'. This was to cause some confusion in identifying the aeroplanes the division claimed during the aerial combat that ensued. The Japanese were flying in formations of three to four aircraft, making up a large V formation, with at least two of the aeroplanes that Valencia believed were 'Franks' flying up above the main body of enemy fighters. It was the opportunity that he and his division had trained hard for.

French and Smith went into attack first while Valencia and Mitchell stayed above to cover them. Coming in unseen, French and Smith each latched onto one of the 'Franks' leading the formation, firing until their targets exploded – French claimed that his victim was a 'Zeke', while Smith claimed a 'Frank'. As French and Smith pulled up to provide cover for their colleagues, as they had trained to do, Valencia and Mitchell went after two of the fighters flying above the main formation. Valencia fired from close range and saw his target explode as he pulled up and away. Following closely behind, Harris Mitchell flamed the second fighter and then climbed up after Valencia.

After these first attacks the Japanese formation entered a left-hand circle, losing altitude, but continuing south towards the Task Force. Valencia then initiated the 'Mowing Machine' tactic that his division had perfected. While French and Smith provided cover, Valencia and Mitchell dove back into the Japanese fighters, flaming two more, with Valencia claiming a 'Frank' again and Mitchell a 'Zeke'. The two pilots then climbed up to cover French and Smith on their next attack. French flamed what he claimed was his second 'Zeke', while Smith fired at a fighter he identified as a 'Frank', which began to pour smoke, but did not explode – Smith later received credit for a probable. As the Japanese formation began to break apart, Valencia ordered French and Smith to seek their own targets while he and Mitchell did the same.

Flying below Valencia's division, Lt Phillips had not been aware of the approaching Japanese formation until he saw aeroplanes exploding above him. Climbing up to higher altitude to join the fight, Phillips and his three pilots chased after enemy aircraft that were diving away from Valencia's division. The Japanese pilots seemed to be a mix of veterans and poorly trained newcomers, with the former being aggressive and making runs on the Hellcats – they also performed a variety of evasive manoeuvres when attacked. Most, however, resorted to flying a simple tight descending circle to escape. A few Hellcats from other squadrons also joined in the combat to give the two VF-9 divisions some support.

Valencia and Mitchell had continued making runs on individual aircraft and small formations. Valencia closed in on one fighter he thought was a 'Frank', opening fire at just 100 yards. The Japanese aeroplane began smoking and, as the pilot turned to escape, his fighter blew up. Having just claimed his third victory, Valencia went after a formation of three fighters. He became momentarily distracted, however, when tracers went flying past his aeroplane but failed to hit him. With Mitchell flying behind him, Valencia focused on the formation once again. He fired at one of the three aircraft while Mitchell went after another, the Hellcat pilots following their opponents in a tight turn. Both Japanese fighters burst into flame, Valencia claiming his as a 'Frank', while Mitchell, firing at the same formation, was credited with his third 'Zeke'.

Valencia immediately went after the third aeroplane in the formation, closing in to set the Japanese fighter on fire. The aircraft exploded as it sought to get away, giving Valencia his fifth kill of the engagement. Pulling up from his last attack, he saw a Japanese fighter closing on two Hellcats below him. Diving down, Valencia closed in on the aeroplane (which he identified as yet another 'Frank') and fired until it too blew up. In his last combat, Valencia fired on a smoking fighter that went past him, sending it down pouring even more smoke. Crucially, however, he did not see it hit the water. On his way back to the carrier, Valencia encountered one more Japanese fighter, but when he manoeuvred into position and pressed the gun button he found that he was out of ammunition.

Landing back aboard *Yorktown*, Valencia's division toted up the score. Valencia had claimed six 'Franks' destroyed, one probable and one damaged, Harris Mitchell had claimed three 'Zekes' destroyed and a fourth as a probable, Jim French was credited with four 'Zekes' and Clinton Smith claimed one 'Frank' and another as a probable. Harris Mitchell and John French both became aces on this mission. Phillips' division contributed

Lt Eugene Valencia's division had another successful day on 4 May 1945, claiming 11.5 Japanese aircraft shot down. Valencia himself claimed 3.5 victories, Harris Mitchell and James French three each and Clinton Smith claimed two *(80G-376171, NARA)*

another three kills, giving VF-9 a total of 17 for the day. For his leadership and accomplishment on this mission, Valencia was awarded the Navy Cross.

For the next two weeks VF-9 continued to fly CAPs mixed with strikes against targets on Okinawa. The squadron claimed only one Japanese aircraft by day, however – a Nakajima C6N carrier reconnaissance aeroplane ('Myrt') shot down on 22 April. The nightfighter flight had better luck, with future ace Ens John Orth claiming an 'Irving' and a 'Betty' shot down in the early hours of 30 April while on a night CAP over the Task Force. The IJN regularly sent out 'Irving' reconnaissance aircraft and 'Betty' bombers to try to locate TF 58 for the next day's attacks, the latter aircraft occasionally launching night torpedo attacks.

Orth was vectored onto a small formation of four twin-engined aeroplanes flying at 1000 ft, with an 'Irving', its wing and tail lights on, leading the other three – Orth identified one of these as a 'Betty'. He closed on the 'Irving' and set it on fire with three short bursts from directly behind. The 'Irving' rolled over and crashed into the sea. Orth quickly swung in behind the 'Betty' and opened fire, hitting the wing fuel tanks. The bomber burst into flames and rolled first to the right and then to the left, before hitting the water with a giant explosion that temporarily blinded Orth.

On 4 May VF-9 had another red letter day – its best of the entire Okinawa campaign. The scoring began in the early hours with the nightfighter flight. At 0200 hrs Lt Dale Knopf shot down a Kawanishi H8K 'Emily' flying boat that was searching for the Task Force. At 0300 hrs, Ens John Orth took off on a dawn CAP over the Task Force. In the space of two hours he achieved the remarkable feat of shooting down three 'Betty' bombers in his F6F-5N. Orth was given a vector to take station in the northwest sector, but before he arrived at this point the fighter director aboard USS *Randolph* (CV-15) gave him a series of vectors that led him to his first target.

Dropping his gear and flaps to slow his Hellcat down as he came in behind the contact, Orth then pulled them up again when he had slowed down sufficiently. Identifying his target as a 'Betty', Orth fired and set the bomber's port engine alight. The bomber immediately dived away, rolling

Ens John Orth was VF-9's solitary nightfighter ace, and he claimed his first victory on 5 April 1945. On 4 May 1945 (VF-9's most successful day on its third combat cruise in terms of aerial victories) Orth shot down three 'Betty' bombers during the course of a single night mission – a feat that not only made him an ace but also earned him the Navy Cross (*via the author*)

Deck crews re-spot Hellcats on board *Yorktown* between missions. Aeroplanes moved back and forth constantly before and after missions. As previously noted, US Navy carrier pilots did not have their own individual aircraft, but flew whichever aeroplane they were assigned for a particular mission. During the Okinawa campaign fighter pilots on *Essex*-class carriers often flew as many as 50 different Hellcats (*80G-333405, NARA*)

Yorktown, which was home to CAG-9 during the Okinawa campaign (*80G-438766, NARA*)

left and right. Orth dropped his gear and flaps again to stay with the 'Betty' and, as it fell, the flames enveloped the bomber's left wing and it hit the water and exploded. Climbing up, Orth was given another series of vectors leading him to a second 'Betty' bomber. Again coming in from behind, he closed in and opened fire from 200-300 ft, getting hits on the port engine and both wing roots. The 'Betty' pushed over into a dive and Orth followed, getting in two more bursts and sending the aeroplane down into the water.

Climbing back up to 8000 ft, Orth orbited until *Randolph* gave him a third vector. This turned out to be his third 'Betty' of the night, flying above him at 13,000 ft. Visually acquiring his quarry from a quarter-of-a-mile away, Orth once again pulled up behind the 'Betty' and opened fire at close range. Both engines immediately caught fire and the bomber dove into the sea and exploded. This combat made John Orth one of only four US Navy nightfighter aces, with six victories to his name, and earned him the Navy Cross.

Fifteen minutes after Orth had scored his last victory at 0455 hrs, Eugene Valencia led his and two other divisions off on a CAP over destroyers manning Radar Picket Station No 1, due north of Okinawa. Lt Bert Eckard led the second division and Lt(jg) James Caldwell the third. Arriving on station at around 0600 hrs, Valencia's division climbed to 20,000 ft to orbit, while Caldwell orbited below at 12,000 ft and Eckard at 8000 ft.

The VF-9 pilots aloft that morning were totally oblivious to the fact that the Imperial Japanese Headquarters had scheduled the fifth Kikusui mission for 4 May to coincide with a Japanese Army counterattack on Okinawa. The JAAF sent off around 50 Special Attack aeroplanes with an escort of 35 'Franks', while the IJN marshalled 75 Special Attack aeroplanes with an escort of 48 Zero-sens and 35 'George' fighters. These formations were headed directly for Okinawa.

Bert Eckard's division relieved Valencia's at 0715 hrs, the latter pilot leading his pilots down to 8000 ft. Soon both he and Harris Mitchell received a vector and duly headed north, leaving Jim French and Clinton Smith to continue to orbit. Valencia found no aeroplanes at altitude, but as he and Mitchell were returning to their station they saw a lone Ki-46 'Dinah' flying with a 'Frank' at 3000 ft. Valencia went after the fighter and had a narrow escape, as the After Action Report recorded;

'Valencia made a stern run on the "Frank", spraying it with two long bursts. The "Frank" burst into flames under the cockpit, and as Valencia passed over it he saw the pilot raise himself up in the cockpit, look back and then up at him, get back into the cockpit and then pull the "Frank" up sharply in an attempt to ram Valencia's aeroplane, which Valencia avoided by pulling up very violently.'

The 'Frank' crashed into the water. Mitchell went after the 'Dinah', closing in on his target as it flew just above the waves. He decided to try

Individual markings on US Navy fighters were rare at this time. Indeed, this was one of the few Hellcats on *Yorktown* that had an individual touch in the form of a pin-up girl from a Vargas calendar painted on by a plane captain (*80G-320134, NARA*)

As the deck crew start to remove the chocks, a pilot prepares to taxi his Hellcat forward to launch on another CAP (*80G-333365, NARA*)

for a 'One Slug' McWhorter shot, firing only his two inboard machine guns. Barely touching the trigger, he hit the 'Dinah' in the right wing with a short burst. The Ki-46 did a half-roll and Mitchell fired another short burst, sending the 'Dinah' crashing into the water.

Soon after Valencia and Mitchell rejoined French and Smith over the radar picket ships, Japanese Kamikaze aircraft and their escorts began attacking the vessels, coming in singly or in small groups under a thin layer of clouds. Seeing five 'Vals' approaching, Valencia made a head-on run on one of them, raking its fuselage. The 'Val' exploded before Valencia could make another run at it. Returning to their station, Valencia and Mitchell saw more 'Vals' heading towards the ships. Valencia made a stern attack on another 'Val', getting hits on its tail and fuselage. The aeroplane rolled over and went straight down into the sea. Valencia then attacked a 'Frank' that was making a bombing run on one of the destroyers. The vessel's guns had already hit the aircraft, for it was trailing smoke as it made its bombing run. Several other Hellcats shot at the Japanese fighter too, but Valencia downed it with a head-on run – he later received a half-credit for its destruction.

Mitchell, meanwhile, had gone after another 'Frank' that was heading for the picket ships, closing until he was just behind the fighter before opening fire. Both wings on the 'Frank' burst into flames and the aeroplane hit the water and blew up. Circling above the ships, Mitchell saw yet another 'Frank' commencing a run on a destroyer. The VF-9 ace targeted the JAAF fighter with a 75-degree deflection shot that hit its engine and fuselage. The 'Frank' started burning, but continued its dive towards the ship, fortunately crashing just beyond it.

Jim French and Clinton Smith were having their own battles. As the former came in behind an 'Oscar', the Japanese pilot lowered his wheels in an attempt to force French to overshoot, but the Naval Aviator quickly dropped the wheels of his own fighter and opened fire. The 'Oscar' pulled up and over one of the destroyers – its intended target – and crashed into the water. Seeing a 'Frank' beginning a loop, French climbed up after it, but found he had only one gun firing. He hastily charged his remaining weapons, dropped his flaps, gave the 'Frank' sufficient lead and opened fire, getting hits on the wings and in the cockpit area. The enemy pilot performed a 'split-S' and crashed straight into the water.

Clinton Smith had fired at several aeroplanes before latching onto a 'Frank' that he spotted diving on one of the ships. The fighter dropped its bombs and then made a sharp turn, but Smith followed and hit the 'Frank' with a long burst. The Japanese fighter rolled over and flew into the water. Smith continued to cover the picket ships, and ten minutes later he saw a 'Judy' coming in low over the water. Two other friendly fighters shot at the dive-bomber but missed, so Smith came in low directly on its tail and fired three long bursts, setting the aeroplane on fire. The 'Judy' rolled over and also crashed into the water. French made the last kill for the division when Valencia pulled in behind a 'Nate', only to find that he was out of ammunition. Valencia radioed French, who came in and destroyed the 'Nate' with a single burst of fire.

Valencia, Mitchell and Smith all had to land on Yontan airfield, on Okinawa, in order to refuel, Smith discovering that he had only ten gallons left in his tanks upon shutting down. Valencia's division claimed 11.5 aircraft during the battle.

Bert Eckard shot down a 'Val' for his second victory of the war whilst defending the picket ships, and three more pilots claimed single kills.

Three other VF-9 divisions also ran into Japanese aeroplanes that morning. At 0630 hrs, Lt Marvin Franger led 12 fighters on a CAP, being told to fly to Radar Picket Station No 14 northwest of Okinawa. Once there, Lt Edward McGowan's division was vectored north, but it found nothing. Returning to their station, McGowan spotted enemy aircraft targeting ships at Radar Picket Station No 1 and led his division in to give support to Valencia and his pilots.

As he approached the picket ships, McGowan saw a 'Tojo' flying below him at 3000 ft. He closed in on the fighter's tail and opened fire. The Japanese pilot's only evasive action was to enter a shallow dive as McGowan continued to fire, hitting the Ki-44 in the fuselage and cockpit. The 'Tojo' began to smoke as it continued to descend, then burst into flames and crashed into the sea. After pursuing several other aircraft, only to see them shot down in front of him, McGowan saw an 'Oscar' beyond the picket ships and latched onto its tail some 200 ft above the water. The pilot of the Ki-43 attempted a tight turn, but McGowan followed and hit it in the engine and fuselage. The 'Oscar' rolled over onto its back and went in. These two kills, his last victories of the war, made McGowan an ace. Two other pilots from his division claimed single kills during this battle, while the two divisions covering Radar Picket Station No 14 scored an additional three victories.

The third fight that morning took place to the north of Okinawa. Lt Howard Hudson had taken his division to attack the airfield on Kikai Island, after which he was to patrol over both Kikai and Amami Islands. Hudson and his pilots, flying camera-equipped F6F-5Ps, had also been given the added responsibility of taking photographs of damage inflicted during the attack. The four pilots dropped their bombs on the runway and then continued to patrol the area. When the next division arrived, Hudson and his wingman, Lt(jg) William McLaurin, went back on a photo run over the airfield, while his second section – Lt(jg) Henry Champion leading Ens Howard Hudspeth – went looking for Japanese aircraft.

Flying 15 miles north of Amami, Champion spotted two 'Jake' floatplanes flying at 500 ft above the water. These were most likely part of a Special Attack force of seaplanes sent out as part of Kikusui No 5 that morning. Champion came in behind the first 'Jake' and shot it down with hits in the wing roots, setting the aeroplane on fire. Hudspeth then attacked the second 'Jake', although he only hit it a few times in the tail during his first pass. Champion came around again and fired, striking the cockpit and the wing. The 'Jake' burst into flames and exploded just as Champion flew over it. From the force of the explosion, it is probable that the bomb the 'Jake' was carrying had detonated. Being just 100 ft from the floatplane when it exploded, the Hellcat had had its wings and tailplane buckled. The fuselage had also been liberally peppered with shrapnel. Champion limped back to the carrier and landed, where his aeroplane was subsequently jettisoned over the side of *Yorktown*.

After making their photo run over the airfield, Hudson and McLaurin saw a melee nearby and rushed over to find friendly fighters in combat with eight to ten 'Georges' and 'Zekes' – probably part of the escort for the Special Attack aeroplanes of Kikusui No 5. McLaurin made a high-side run on a 'Zeke', setting its engine on fire and sending it diving straight down towards the ground.

Rejoining Hudson, McLaurin found a 'George' on his tail. The enemy fighter's 20 mm fire hit his wings, fuselage and tail, knocking out his radio equipment and hitting his seat back armour plating. Coming to the rescue of his wingman, Hudson quickly turned on the 'George', forcing its pilot to break away. The latter proved to be an unusually aggressive opponent, however, coming right back after the two Hellcats in a head-on run. He aimed his fire under Hudson's aeroplane at McLaurin's damaged F6F. Hudson entered a turn, and kept turning, until he was on the 'George's' tail. Opening fire from the 'eight o'clock' position, he hit the fighter's engine and cockpit. The 'George' began smoking, and it soon crashed into the sea.

In total, VF-9 pilots had claimed 30.5 Japanese aircraft shot down on 4 May 1945.

One week later the Japanese launched Kikusui No 6, sending 150 Special Attack aircraft with escorts against American shipping around Okinawa over 10-11 May. The actions on the 11th turned out to be VF-9's last big aerial combat of the war.

At 0645 hrs Lt Eugene Valencia led his division on VF-9's second CAP of the morning, with Lts Marvin Franger and Bert Eckard leading their divisions. As they arrived on station, *Yorktown's* fighter director sent Valencia's division to orbit over Yoron Shima, northeast of Okinawa, Franger's division 20 miles to the north and Eckard's division 30 miles to the west to orbit over Izena Shima.

Valencia's division was the first to go into action when, at around 0800 hrs, he and his pilots spotted a mixed formation of eight JAAF fighters approaching. Identifying them as 'Tonys', 'Oscars', 'Franks' and 'Tojos', Valencia ordered Jim French and Clinton Smith to go after the four aeroplanes leading the formation while he engaged two machines he had seen coming out of the sun. The division soon got separated, although French and Smith managed to stay together.

Climbing up towards the fighters above him, Valencia soon recognised them as F6Fs. However, moments later he saw a lone 'Tony' shoot down one of the Hellcats. Another Ki-61 then broke away from a second

formation above the remaining Grumman fighter and started attacking it too. Valencia went after this machine, whose pilot manoeuvred violently in an attempt to escape. Valencia eventually found himself coming in head-on at the 'Tony', and with several long bursts knocked a large section of the fighter's wing off. The Ki-61 dropped away out of control.

Climbing back up, Valencia spotted an 'Oscar' above him and attacked it, hitting the Japanese fighter in the cockpit area and wing roots and sending it down in flames. Joining up with two other F6Fs, Valencia attacked a Japanese fighter that he could not identify. The aeroplane was brownish green in colour, with a radial engine, a long canopy and an extended tail wheel – it was possibly a Kawasaki Ki-100-I fighter, which was little known by the Allies at the time. Coming in on a flat-side run from 'seven o'clock', Valencia fired on the Japanese fighter and hit the engine, which exploded. The aircraft then spun down out of control.

Harris Mitchell was climbing up with Valencia towards the original JAAF fighter formation when three 'Tonys' jumped him. Forced to perform a 'split-S' to escape, Mitchell was unable to rejoin Valencia in the mix of Japanese and American aeroplanes that were fighting each other. Instead, he went after several Ki-61s that were being attacked by Corsairs, getting on the tail of one 'Tony' and exploding the Japanese fighter with hits on its wings and fuselage. After trying to rejoin his division, Mitchell saw another Ki-61 attempting to bounce him from behind. He turned to get onto the 'Tony's' tail and ended up pursuing the fighter in a long chase at full power with water injection before getting close enough to bring it down.

French and Smith had attacked the first formation that Valencia had spotted, French shooting down an 'Oscar' and then going after a pair of 'Franks' that he saw diving down below him. He fired on one of the fighters, setting its engine on fire and sending it crashing in flames. French quickly went after the second 'Frank', which passed in front of his

Hellcats on board *Yorktown* in late May or early June 1945 prepare to launch. After a brief rest at Ulithi, the Task Group returned to the area around Okinawa, where VF-9 continued to fly CAPs and strikes against airfields on Kyushu (*80G-333364, NARA*)

gunsight. Firing from directly astern, he set this 'Frank' on fire too for his third claim of the day. French and Smith then linked back up with Valencia and came across a 'Frances' bomber intent on attacking one of the picket ships. Smith went after the IJN machine, which was flying so low over the water that it was difficult for him to bring his guns to bear. Smith set the port engine on fire and the 'Frances' crashed into the sea just 1000 yards from the picket ship it was targeting.

Bert Eckard and his division were flying over their assigned station when they saw a formation of seven 'Zekes' flying slightly above him at 20,000 ft. As the division climbed after them, Eckard's section leader broke off to go after another lower formation. When Eckard and his wingman, Ens Joseph Kaelin, neared the first formation of 'Zekes' they were astonished to find that the seven aeroplanes they had seen were part of a larger formation of 30 to 35 A6Ms. Eckard and Kaelin approached the formation from the rear and targeted several 'Zekes' that were straggling behind the main body of aircraft at the rear of the formation. Eckard initially shot a fighter off Kaelin's tail, and then he and his wingman proceeded to make repeated runs against the 'Zeke' formation, climbing up after each attack to maintain an altitude advantage. The Japanese fighters reacted with various turning manoeuvres, but made no attempt at a coordinated attack against their pursuers. Over the next 20 minutes Eckard shot down five 'Zekes' and damaged a sixth, all with stern attacks from above or at the same level.

While protecting his leader and knocking a fighter off his tail, Kaelin came in on the straggling 'Zekes' with Eckard and claimed three shot down, one probably shot down and two more damaged.

By the end of the combat Eckard and Kaelin had both become aces. They had begun the engagement with two victories apiece, Kaelin having claimed his second kill the day before. These were their last victories of the war. For their achievements, both Eckard and Kaelin were awarded the Navy Cross.

Marvin Franger's division seemed to miss both of the big clashes, however. Seeing a solitary 'Tony', he and his pilots set off in pursuit of the JAAF fighter. Coming in behind it, Franger fired first and saw hits around its cockpit. The 'Tony' fell away and spun down into the sea for Franger's ninth, and last, kill of the war.

In total, the three divisions claimed 20 Japanese aircraft destroyed, another pilot claimed one more victory later in the day to give VF-9 21 claims for 11 May 1945 – the unit's third most successful day of its third combat cruise. These were the last claims credited to Valencia's 'Flying Circus', as his division had come to be called. Months of intensive training had paid off. Valencia, Mitchell, French and Smith had perfected what later became known as 'fluid four' tactics. Together, they had claimed 42.5 Japanese aeroplanes shot down during VF-9's third combat cruise,

Ens Joseph Kaelin (left) and his division leader Lt Bert Eckard. The latter joined VF-9 in January 1945, having previously served with VF-11 and VGS-11, while Kaelin was on his first combat cruise. On 11 May 1945 they attacked a formation of 30 to 35 'Zekes', claiming eight shot down between them (*via the author*)

making Valencia's 'Flying Circus' the highest scoring division in the US Navy. Gene Valencia ended the war tied with Lt Cecil Harris as the US Navy's second- and third-highest scoring aces, and the second-highest scoring Hellcat ace after Cdr David McCampbell.

VF-9's final aerial combats of the war came during the first week of June, and produced the squadron's last two aces. On 3 June Lt Howard Hudson and his photo division accompanied six other divisions from VF-9 and two from VF-46, embarked in *Independence*, on a fighter sweep and strafing attack against airfields in southern Kyushu, to the east of Kagoshima Bay. After the attack on the airfield at Kanoya, Hudson and his division went in for their photo runs, then headed southeast toward the other airfield targets. Southeast of Kanoya, two Japanese fighters jumped them, coming down from 9000 ft in a head-on run against the division's second section, which was flying at 7000 ft. Having identified these fighters as a 'Frank' and a 'Zeke', Lt(jg) William Brewer, Hudson's wingman, went after the latter, getting hits in its engine and wings. The fighter, which went down trailing smoke and with its propeller windmilling, was in a diving turn at 200 ft when Brewer lost sight of it.

The second aircraft was not a 'Frank', but a 'George' – another case of confusing the IJN machine with the JAAF fighter. PO1/c Kiyoshi Miyamoto, from the Sento 407th Hikotai of the 343rd Kokutai, had taken off that morning with 27 other Shiden Kai to intercept the American carrier fighters striking the Japanese airfields on Kyushu. Miyamoto missed his intended target and flew past Hudson's division. Hudson gave chase, and after 15 miles pulled behind Miyamoto and opened fire.

These CAG-9 pilots were flown to Guam on 19 May 1945 to relate their recent combat experiences to the press. Lt Eugene Valencia, Lt Cdr Herbert Houck and a VT-9 pilot listen to Lt Bert Eckard describe his successful combat of 11 May (*80G-329439, NARA*)

Miyamoto did a wingover to escape, but Hudson followed him, firing, and getting hits in the cockpit and setting the left wing on fire. Miyamoto's fighter crashed into Kagoshima Bay for Hudson's fourth victory.

Three days later Hudson became an ace during a CAP over radar picket ships west of Okinawa near Aguni Shima when four 'Tonys' came in from the north intent on hitting the vessels. Lt(jg) McLaurin, Hudson's wingman, shot down one Ki-61, while Lt(jg) Henry Champion, leading Hudson's second section, shot down another in a curving attack for his fourth victory. Hudson went after a third 'Tony' that another F6F and an F4U were chasing, but overshooting. Hudson came down on the Ki-61 and hit its wings and fuselage, the battered fighter rolling over at 400 ft and diving into the sea.

Lt(jg)s Henry Champion and William Brewer made VF-9's last claims on 8 June while on another photo coverage sortie. That morning Lt Cdr Houck led six divisions from VF-9 and five divisions from VBF-9, along with 44 fighters from USS *Ticonderoga* (CV-14), against airfields on southern Kyushu. Lt Howard Hudson was leading his photo division, which was to get post-strike imagery. After the strikes went in, Hudson flew over two of the airfields attacked near Kanoya and then returned to the rendezvous point. Champion and Brewer continued on to cover Shibushi airfield, on Ariake Bay to the east. What followed was, as Champion recalled, his severest test of the entire war;

'Seems like 30+ "Zekes" jumped me and Brewer, who was flying the photo aeroplane, We were really scrambling trying to get out of there. Strangely enough they never hit either one of us, but there was one on each of our tails at all times. We were weaving like mad, turning inside out trying to evade them. Finally, we decided we were going to get it, so we headed for the sea out toward where a life guard submarine was. They broke off when they got to the beach and didn't follow us on out.'

Both pilots had been jumped by a 'Tony' after they had made their photo run over Shibushi airfield at 10,000 ft, the fighter diving out of a bank of clouds. It then broke away, but moments later a 'Frank' attacked them from the same cloud cover, followed by two 'Zekes' and then two more A6Ms that proceeded to make repeated runs against Champion and

Lt Howard Hudson and his division. The Naval Aviators are, from left to right, Lt(jg) William McLaurin, Hudson, Lt(jg) Henry Champion and Ens Howard Hudspeth. Howard Hudson became an ace on 6 June 1945 and Henry Champion joined him two days later. They were the last two VF-9 pilots to achieve this distinction (*via the author*)

The crew of *Yorktown* bid farewell to CAG-9 shortly after the Carrier Air Group had flown its last combat mission on 9 June 1945. Lt Cdr Frank Lawlor, commander of VBF-9, is addressing the crowd, while behind him on the left Lt Jack Kitchen, CO of VF-9, holds a cake (*80G-376296, NARA*)

Brewer. As the After Action Report recorded, 'the Jap pilots coordinated their attacks well, used their speed to climb back up and regain their altitude advantage. They were very aggressive'.

Champion and Brewer immediately began weaving, but found that on some runs two Japanese fighters would bracket them while a third came in on them. This forced the Naval Aviators to tighten up their turns even more, only to find themselves getting out of position to continue their

After the end of the combat cruise, Lt Eugene Valencia and his division posed for publicity shots with a scoreboard showing their combined total of victories against Japanese aircraft, including Valencia's claims from VF-9's second combat cruise. These pilots are, from left to right, Lt(jg) Harris Mitchell, Valencia, Lt(jg) Clinton Smith and Lt(jg) James French (*80GK-5990, NARA*)

weaving. These tactics indicated that the Japanese pilots involved in this action had a good understanding of American defensive tactics. Despite remaining at full power, the tightness of their turns slowed them down to the point where they risked stalling.

Brewer eventually shot down a 'Zeke' as it passed overhead after its run, setting the fighter on fire with hits in the engine and the wings. Champion damaged another 'Zeke', firing at it while he was on his back. As a third A6M began a run on them, Champion turned into the Japanese fighter and fired, hitting the 'Zeke' in the engine and the cockpit and sending it down in flames. This was Champion's fifth kill, making him an ace, although it seems unlikely the knowledge of this achievement registered with him at the time. The two Hellcat pilots slowly worked their way toward Ariake Bay, at which point they dove away and, as Champion recalled, the 'Zekes' did not follow. Champion and Brewer were exceptionally lucky their opponents had been such poor shots.

THE END

VF-9 flew its last mission of World War 2 on 9 June 1945, escorting VB-9 and VT-9 in an attack on Minami Daito Island to the east of Okinawa – anti-aircraft gun emplacements were targeted with napalm bombs, and then strafed. After completing the strikes, TF 38 (having been re-designated on 27 May after Adm William Halsey and Vice Adm John McCain had taken over from Adm Spruance and Vice Adm Mitscher) sailed for Leyte Gulf for rest and refitting. On arrival, CAG-9 received the welcome news that CAG-88 would replace it aboard *Yorktown* and the men of the Carrier Air Group would be heading home. CAG-9 transferred to *Hornet* for the voyage to Pearl Harbor and then on to San Francisco, arriving in California on 8 July 1945.

Lt Eugene Valencia poses next to the cockpit of a Hellcat marked up with his wartime total of 23 victories after the end of VF-9's combat cruise. What appears to be the squadron's insignia is painted just to the right of the victory markings

During its third combat cruise VF-9 had amassed an impressive record, claiming 128.75 Japanese aeroplanes destroyed in the air, with an additional 18 probably destroyed and 52 damaged. In strafing attacks on Japanese airfields, the squadron claimed 47 aeroplanes destroyed, 58 probably destroyed and 209 damaged. Ten VF-9 pilots had become aces during the third combat cruise, either destroying five or more aircraft, or adding to earlier claims from the second combat cruise. VF-9 ended the war with a total of 256.75 aerial victories and 171 aeroplanes destroyed on the ground. The squadron's 20 aces placed it fourth in the ranking of US Navy squadrons, but third in the ranking of Hellcat squadrons.

VF-9 was disestablished in October 1945. The squadron's number had a brief return to life when VF-20 was re-designated VF-9A in November 1946, only to be re-designated VF-91 in August 1948. Fighting Squadron Nine duly faded into history.

APPENDICES

F6F Hellcat Aces of VF-9

Name and Final Rank with VF-9	Score with VF-9	Wartime Total
Lt Eugene Valencia	23	23
Lt(jg) James French	11	11
Lt(jg) Hamilton McWhorter	10	12
Lt(jg) Harris Mitchell	10	10
Lt Marvin Franger	9	9
Lt William Bonneau	8	8
Lt Mayo Hadden	8	8
Lt(jg) Louis Menard	8	9
Lt Bert Eckard	7	7
Lt Edward McGowan	6.5	6.5
Lt Leslie DeCew	6	6
Lt Cdr Herbert Houck	6	6
Ens John Orth	6	6
Lt Armistead Smith	6	10
Lt Clinton Smith	6	6
Lt(jg) Henry Champion	5	5
Ens John Franks	5	7
Lt Howard Hudson	5	5
Ens Joseph Kaelin	5	5
Lt(jg) Albert Martin	5	5

COLOUR PLATES

1
F2A-3 Buffalo (BuNo unknown)/black 9-F-6 of VF-9, East Field, NAS Norfolk, Virginia, March 1942
The Brewster Buffalo was the first aircraft assigned to VF-9 on its establishment. The squadron began with five F2A-3s, all of which had previously served with VS-201 aboard the escort carrier USS *Long Island* (CVE-1). It lost one, BuNo 01581, in a fatal crash just 12 days after being established. In early April F4F-3 Wildcats began to replace the Buffalos. The markings shown here are representative of US Navy markings and camouflage at the time.

2
F4F-4 Wildcat (BuNo unknown)/black 9-F-2 of VF-9, USS *Ranger* (CV-4), August–September 1942
The first F4F-4s arrived in late June 1942 to replace the fixed-wing F4F-3 as Grumman's production of the 'Dash-4' increased. Pilots appreciated the heavier armament of the improved Wildcat, but not its less nimble performance. VF-9 used this particular aeroplane during its work-up cruises from Norfolk to Quonset Point aboard *Ranger* in August and September 1942.

3
F4F-4 Wildcat BuNo 11762/black 9-F-15 flown by Ens Louis Menard, VF-9, USS *Ranger* (CV-4), November 1942
To avoid misidentification during the North African invasion in November 1942, a yellow surround was added to the national insignia on the fuselage and beneath the wings of USAAF and US Navy aircraft involved in the operation. Future ace Ens Louis Menard was flying this aircraft when he claimed a Vichy French Curtiss Hawk H-75 destroyed and a second one as a probable victory inland from Fedala on 9 November 1942. Menard and fellow future ace Marvin Franger were among the few US Navy pilots with claims against two Axis air forces.

4
F6F-3 Hellcat (BuNo unknown)/white 1 flown by Lt Cdr John Raby, VF-9, USS *Essex* (CV-9), February 1943
The first F6F-3 Hellcats were finished in the early war two-tone Blue Gray and Light Gray camouflage scheme as seen here. VF-9 had a practice on its first and second combat cruises of assigning the number '1' to the squadron commander's aircraft, although in practice the CO flew whichever aircraft was available at the time. Lt Cdr John Raby used this aeroplane to make the first landing of a Hellcat aboard *Essex* on 17 February 1943.

5

F6F-3 Hellcat (BuNo unknown)/white 14 of VF-9, USS *Essex* (CV-9), August 1943

Before entering combat, VF-9 received F6F-3 Hellcats that had been painted in the revised three-tone Non-specular Sea Blue, Intermediate Blue and White camouflage scheme depicted in this profile. For the Marcus Island raid on 31 August 1943 the squadron's Hellcats sported large national insignia outlined in red on their fuselages.

6

F6F-3 Hellcat (BuNo unknown)/white 24 of VF-9, USS *Essex* (CV-9), September 1943

Sometime after the Marcus Island raid, VF-9 began painting a small representation of its squadron insignia beneath the cockpit of its Hellcats. The squadron called itself the 'Cat o'Nines' (and also the 'Hellcats'), which was a play on the squadron number and the old 'Cat o'Nine Tails' whip. The insignia featured a cat sitting on a cloud, about to throw a bottle of whisky down on an unsuspecting enemy.

7

F6F-3 Hellcat (BuNo unknown)/white 17 of VF-9, USS *Essex* (CV-9), October 1943

The red border to the national insignia was instituted in June 1943 and then ordered to be removed, at least officially, in September. Photographs indicate that its removal did not happen immediately, however. While the identity of the Naval Aviator who flew this aircraft remains unknown, it was indeed one of the fighters used by VF-9 pilots that claimed the unit's first aerial successes during the attack on Wake Island on 5 October 1943 – note the kill symbol applied beneath the fighter's cockpit to the right of the VF-9 insignia.

8

F6F-3 Hellcat BuNo 25900/white 7 flown by Lt(jg) Hamilton McWhorter, VF-9, USS *Essex* (CV-9), October 1943

Lt(jg) Hamilton 'Big Mac' McWhorter made history in this aircraft when he achieved his fifth victory (a 'Betty' bomber) on 19 November 1943, thereby becoming the first US Navy pilot to become an ace flying the Hellcat. Having used only 87 rounds to down the 'Betty', McWhorter was given the nickname 'One Slug'. He may have had the aeroplane marked with his five victories, as seen here, as VF-9 did mark some of its Hellcats up with kill markings during this second combat cruise.

9

F6F-3 Hellcat BuNo 40509/white 15 flown by Lt(jg) Hamilton McWhorter, VF-9, USS *Essex* (CV-9), January 1944

Lt(jg) Hamilton McWhorter used this aeroplane to shoot down two 'Hamps' during the 29 January 1944 raid on Roi Island. He had the good fortune to have the two IJN fighters literally 'pop up' directly in front of him, allowing McWhorter to close in on them and open fire unseen.

10

F6F-3 Hellcat BuNo 09010/white 26 flown by Lt(jg) Marvin Franger, VF-9, USS *Essex* (CV-9), January 1944

On the 29 January 1944 mission against Roi, Lt(jg) Marvin Franger shot down a 'Hamp' and a 'Zeke' with this aircraft for his third and fourth kills. Franger, along with squadronmate Louis Menard, was one of only a handful of US Navy aces to claim victories during three combat cruises. Franger made three claims (one destroyed, one probable and one damaged) over North Africa in 1942, five claims (all victories) against Japanese aircraft during VF-9's second combat cruise in 1943-44 and four claims (three kills and one damaged)

during the third combat cruise, scoring his last victory on 11 May 1945 – 31 months after his first victory. During his tours Franger made claims against eight different types of aircraft.

11

F6F-3 Hellcat (BuNo unknown)/white 27 flown by Lt(jg) Eugene Valencia, VF-9, USS *Essex* (CV-9), January 1944

Lt(jg) Eugene Valencia used this aircraft to shoot down a fighter he claimed as an 'Oscar' on 29 January 1944 during the attack on Roi, this victory taking his total to 4.5 kills. His victim was more likely to have been an A6M3 Model 32 'Hamp', as the JAAF had no aircraft stationed in the Central Pacific – the IJN was responsible for all aircraft operations in this area during World War 2.

12

F6F-3 Hellcat (BuNo unknown)/white 35 flown by Lt Leslie DeCew, VF-9, USS *Essex* (CV-9), January 1944

Lt Leslie DeCew shot down a 'Zeke' in this aeroplane during the Roi attack on 29 January 1944. DeCew was another long-serving VF-9 pilot, completing two combat cruises with the squadron after having spent his first year in the US Navy as a flying instructor. He just missed 'making ace' during the squadron's second combat cruise, claiming four Japanese aeroplanes shot down. DeCew had to wait 14 months to get his fifth and sixth victories (and a further two fighters damaged), which he claimed during the 16 February 1945 strike on Tokyo.

13

F6F-3 Hellcat (BuNo unknown)/white 36 flown by Lt(jg) William Bonneau, VF-9, USS *Essex* (CV-9), February 1944

Lt(jg) William Bonneau shot down a 'Zeke' and three 'Rufes' in this aeroplane during a fierce dogfight over Truk on 17 February 1944, these successes taking his tally to seven kills overall. Bill Bonneau and Eugene Valencia were close friends, having known each other before the war when they owned an aeroplane together. Like Valencia, Bonneau was commissioned in February 1942, but was assigned to VF-9 in April while Valencia became a flight instructor. When the latter joined VF-9 in February 1943, he and Bonneau began flying together regularly (they also shared a stateroom on *Essex*), earning them the nickname 'The Flying Twins'. Bonneau scored seven of his eight victories during VF-9's second combat cruise, but by a quirk of fate he had few encounters with Japanese aeroplanes during the Okinawa campaign.

14

F6F-3 Hellcat BuNo 66056/white 22 flown by Lt(jg) Marvin Franger, VF-9, USS *Essex* (CV-9), February 1944

Lt(jg) Marvin Franger 'made ace' in this aircraft on 17 February 1944 when he shot down a 'Zeke' over Truk. US Navy carrier pilots typically did not have their own individually assigned aircraft, instead flying whichever machine was assigned to them for a particular mission. Whilst participating in VF-9's second combat cruise Franger flew at least 25 different Hellcats in combat, including three aeroplanes during the missions to Truk.

15

F6F-3 Hellcat (BuNo unknown)/white 17 flown by Ens John Franks, VF-9, USS *Essex* (CV-9), February 1944

Ens John Franks shot down two 'Zekes' and a 'Pete' in this aeroplane during the strike on Truk on 17 February 1944. Five days later he became an ace when he downed another 'Zeke' flying F6F-3 white 25 over Saipan airfield. Franks was one of a number of VF-9 pilots who left the squadron upon its return to the USA and transferred to VF-12. He shot down two more Japanese aircraft (and damaged a further two) while serving with VF-12 during the unit's 1945 cruise embarked in *Randolph*.

16

F6F-3 Hellcat (BuNo unknown)/white 5 flown by Lt Mayo Hadden, VF-9, USS *Essex* (CV-9), February 1944

Lt Mayo Hadden shot down three 'Zekes' in this aeroplane on 17 February 1944 over Truk to become an ace – seven of his eight victories were Zero-sens. Hadden served with VF-9 during Operation *Torch* and through the squadron's second combat cruise, leaving it after the unit had returned home. Remaining in the US Navy post-war, he spent time on two more *Essex*-class carriers during the post-war years, serving as navigator on board *Yorktown* from July 1956 through to May 1958 and as captain of *Hornet* from July 1964 to July 1965. Hadden retired from the US Navy on 1 July 1973 with the rank of rear admiral.

17

F6F-3 Hellcat (BuNo unknown)/white 25 flown by Lt Cdr Herbert Houck, VF-9, USS *Essex* (CV-9), February 1944

Lt Cdr Herbert Houck shot down a 'Pete' and a 'Kate' in this aeroplane to 'make ace' during the 17 February 1944 raid on Truk. Five days later Ens John Franks claimed his fifth victory in this aircraft on 22 February 1944. One of the few pre-war Naval Aviators in VF-9, Herbert Houck had joined the US Navy in 1936. He served in VS-2 aboard USS *Lexington* (CV-2) and spent a year and a half as a scout aeroplane pilot aboard the cruiser USS *Pensacola* (CA-24) before becoming a flight instructor at NAS Pensacola. After two years of training neophyte Naval Aviators, Houck joined VF-9 in December 1942. He became Executive Officer of the squadron in July 1943, and replaced Lt Cdr Phil Torrey as squadron CO in December of that same year. During the squadron's second combat cruise Houck claimed five victories and was awarded two Navy Crosses for his actions in the strikes on Rabaul and Truk. Taking command of CAG-9 when Torrey was lost over Tokyo on 16 February 1945, Houck was awarded his third Navy Cross for leading the Carrier Air Group in the attack on the IJN battleship *Yamato* on 7 April 1945.

18

F6F-3 Hellcat (BuNo unknown)/white 4 flown by Lt(jg) Howard Hudson, VF-9, USS *Essex* (CV-9), February 1944

Lt(jg) Howard Hudson shot down a 'Kate' in this aeroplane during the 17 February 1944 raid on Truk. Another of the long-serving VF-9 pilots who had to wait until the unit's third combat cruise before they 'made ace', Hudson shot down two 'Kates' during the squadron's second combat cruise but did not get his fifth kill until he claimed a 'Tony' destroyed on 6 June 1945.

19

F6F-3 Hellcat BuNo 40125/white 19 flown by Lt(jg) Hamilton McWhorter, VF-9, USS *Essex* (CV-9), February 1944

Lt(jg) Hamilton McWhorter shot down two 'Zekes' and a 'Hamp' in this aeroplane during the raid on Truk to become the first Hellcat double ace. These were his last victories with VF-9, for after returning to the USA McWhorter spent several months instructing novice fighter pilots and then, with several other veterans of VF-9, helped re-form VF-12. Flying with the latter unit off *Randolph* in 1945, McWhorter made two more kill claims during the February Tokyo strikes and the May Okinawa campaign to end the war with 12 victories and two damaged to his name.

20

F6F-3 Hellcat BuNo 40807/white 13 flown by Lt(jg) Louis Menard, VF-9, USS *Essex* (CV-9), February 1944

Lt(jg) Louis Menard shot down two 'Petes' and two 'Kates' in this aeroplane over Truk to become an ace. Returning to the USA, Menard also joined VF-12 but was then transferred to VBF-12 when the large 72-aeroplane squadrons were split into separate fighter and fighter-bomber units. Menard scored one more victory with VBF-12 during the February 1945 strikes on Tokyo, becoming one of the few US Navy pilots to claim kills on three combat cruises. He was also one of an even smaller number to have achieved victories against two Axis air forces.

21

F6F-3 Hellcat BuNo 04809/white 23 flown by Lt Armistead Smith, VF-9, USS *Essex* (CV-9), February 1944

BuNo 04809 was a lucky aircraft for VF-9 pilots. Lt(jg) Louis Menard shot down a 'Kate' over Roi while flying it on 29 January 1944, and Lt Armistead Smith destroyed three 'Zekes' with it over Truk on 17 February 1944. Photographs show this aeroplane with three Japanese flags under the cockpit, these victory symbols possibly representing Smith's trio of kills at Truk. While pilots did not have their own individual aircraft, it appears that during the second combat cruise VF-9 had a practice of adding a Japanese flag to a Hellcat that had claimed an aircraft destroyed. Smith had 'made ace' during the Truk raid, and he claimed a sixth kill five days later. Like McWhorter and Menard, 'Chick' Smith subsequently joined VBF-12 following his return home. Indeed, he was made the squadron's Executive Officer upon its establishment in January 1945. Smith claimed four more victories flying with VBF-12 to end the war with ten kills and 0.333 damaged.

22

F6F-3 Hellcat (BuNo unknown)/white 21 flown by Lt(jg) Eugene Valencia, VF-9, USS *Essex* (CV-9), February 1944

Lt(jg) Eugene Valencia was another of the VF-9 pilots who became an ace over Truk, shooting down three 'Zekes' in this aeroplane. This mission proved formative for Valencia, his experience fighting against superior numbers of enemy fighters leading to his conclusion that the Japanese had poor and uncoordinated defensive tactics. This led directly to the development of his 'Mowing Machine' tactics, which saw the use of both sections of a division of fighters in a coordinated, but aggressive attack on enemy aircraft.

23

F6F-3 Hellcat BuNo 40011/white 34 flown by Lt(jg) Marvin Franger, VF-9, USS *Essex* (CV-9), February 1944

Lt(jg) Marvin Franger shot down a 'Zeke' in this aeroplane on 22 February 1944 over Saipan for his sixth victory. Having seen the enemy fighter making a run on a division of Hellcats flying high cover for other F6Fs that were strafing the airfield on Saipan, he manoeuvred into a position to make a high-side pass on the 'Zeke'. Firing a long burst that set his target on fire, Franger watched the A6M spin down and crash. He used four different Hellcats to shoot down the five Japanese aircraft he claimed during VF-9's second combat cruise.

24

F6F-3 Hellcat (BuNo unknown)/white 6 flown by Lt(jg) Armistead Smith, VF-9, USS *Essex* (CV-9), February 1944

Lt(jg) Armistead Smith shot down a 'Betty' in this aeroplane on 22 February 1944 over Saipan while on an emergency CAP near *Essex*. With their unprotected fuel tanks in the wings, the 'Betty' bomber was extremely vulnerable to a burst of fire from a Hellcat. Indeed, Smith shot down the aeroplane in a single pass.

25
F6F-3 Hellcat (BuNo unknown)/white 12 of VF-9, USS *Essex* (CV-9), March 1944

VF-9 used this war-weary aeroplane as the mount for several publicity shots that were taken as *Essex* sailed back to Pearl Harbor at the end of VF-9's second combat cruise. Photographs show Lt(jg) George Blair sitting in the cockpit of the fighter with three Japanese flags on the fuselage beneath him representing his three victory claims and Lt(jg) Hamilton McWhorter sat in the same aeroplane with ten Japanese flags for his claims.

26
F6F-5 Hellcat (BuNo unknown)/white 19 flown by Lt Eugene Valencia, VF-9, USS *Lexington* (CV-16), February 1945

VF-9 flew the F6F-5 during its third combat cruise. Embarking on *Lexington* in February 1945, the squadron probably took over the aeroplanes of VF-20 – the unit it replaced aboard the ship. The white band across the tail identified *Lexington* in the geometric system used to identify aircraft assigned to TF 58's carriers from January through to July 1945. With upwards of 72 Hellcats on board vessels operating with the Fast Carrier Task Force, there was little time to add much more than the standard insignia and carrier identification as seen here. The F6F-5 depicted in this profile is one of the rarer examples from the period, as it had victory markings applied beneath the cockpit. This aeroplane was supposedly flown by Lt Eugene Valencia in February 1945, VF-9's ranking ace claiming three victories during the course of that month.

27
F6F-5 Hellcat (BuNo unknown)/white 66 of VF-9, USS *Yorktown* (CV-10), March 1945

When VF-9 moved to *Yorktown* the squadron's Hellcats were repainted with a white diagonal stripe on the fin and rudder as an identifying marking. The white ring around the front of the cowling was added to all squadron aircraft prior to CAG-9 participating in the strikes against targets on Kyushu on 18-19 March 1945.

28
F6F-5 Hellcat (BuNo unknown)/white 3 flown by Lt Eugene Valencia, VF-9, USS *Yorktown* (CV-10), April 1945

This aircraft is thought to have been one of the aeroplanes that Lt Eugene Valencia flew while embarked in *Yorktown*. The fighter's green propeller spinner was another identifying marking unique to aircraft of CV-10. VF-9 and VBF-9 used Hellcats on board the carrier interchangeably. During his three and a half months on board *Yorktown*, Lt(jg) James French flew 37 different Hellcats and used four different aircraft to score his ten victories.

29
F6F-5 Hellcat (BuNo unknown)/white 16 of VF-9, USS *Yorktown* (CV-10), April 1945

White 16 was one of the very few Hellcats to display any kind of personal markings, in this case a pin-up copied from one of the popular Vargas calendars by the aeroplane's crew chief.

30
F6F-5N Hellcat (BuNo unknown)/white N4 flown by Ens John Orth, VF-9, USS *Yorktown* (CV-10), May 1945

Ens John Orth was the high-scoring pilot within VF-9's nightfighter flight, shooting down three 'Betty' bombers in this aeroplane during the early hours of 4 May 1945 to add to the three victories he had attained the previous month. The nightfighter F6F-5Ns often had their white carrier identification markings removed so as to be less visible at night, and some nightfighter flights added an N to the aircraft number as seen here.

Back Cover
F6F-5 Hellcat (BuNo unknown)/white 6? Of VF-9, USS *Yorktown* (CV-10), June 1945

On the way to the Philippines after the end of VF-9's combat tour in June 1945, Eugene Valencia and the members of his division – Harris Mitchell, Jim French and Clinton Smith – posed for a number of publicity photographs, sat on and posing in front of a Hellcat whilst holding a panel showing their combined total of 50 victories. The squadron added 23 Japanese flag victories beneath the cockpit of the F6F-5, these denoting Eugene Valencia's final score. VF-9's ranking ace duly posed next to his record for the camera, although he never flew the Hellcat in combat with these markings applied. Frustratingly, the photograph shows what may only be a partial aircraft identification number.

INDEX